Timber Joints

Edgar (Ted) Stubbersfield

Copyright © 2016 Rachel Stubbersfield

All rights reserved.

ISBN: 0-9944157-4-5
ISBN-13: 978-0-9944157-4-5

DEDICATION

This book is dedicated to Henri Bailleres and his dedicated, hard working and innovative team of scientists and technicians at the Salisbury Research Facility of the Queensland Department of Agriculture and Fisheries.

CONTENTS

	Acknowledgments	Pg. i
	Introduction	Pg. 1
1	Old and New Joints	Pg. 5
2	Galvanised or Stainless Fasteners and Connectors	Pg 13
3	Nails	Pg 26
4	Threaded Fasteners	Pg 36
5	Split Ring Connectors and Shear Plates	Pg 47
6	Nailplates	Pg 60
7	Pressed Metal Connectors	Pg 73
8	Relationship of F Rating to Joint Group	Pg 79
9	Weather Exposed Joints	Pg 81
10	Joints in Glued Beams and Panels	Pg 85
11	Case Histories	Pg 91
	Appendix	Pg 96
	Source of Images	Pg 97
	Works Cited	Pg 100

ACKNOWLEDGMENTS

Oscar Duyvestyn
AECOM

Shane Earle
Queensland Heritage Restorations

Nate Erde-Wollheim.
Portland Bolt

Deputy State Coroner
Coroners Court of Queensland

Derek Folsom
Vermont Timber Works

Paul Gomm
Technical Timber Services Ltd

Andrew Goode
Product Manager, Airco Brands

Chris Hall
Azuma Design Build

Herb Kuhn
Simpson Strong-Tie

Professor Miles Lewis

Zhengwei Li
Branz

Robert Mansell
Hyne

Roger Marks

Will McLean
Galvanisers Association of Australia

Greg Meachem
Timber Insights

Associate Professor Gregory Nolan
University of Tasmania

Owen Peake

Silvia Pugnaloni
Rothoblaas

Damiana Ribiani
Rothoblaas

Stan Sias
Simpson Strong-Tie

Matthew Smith
Multinail

Professor Thomas D. Visser
University of Vermont

Samuel Zelinka
USDA Forest Service

INTRODUCTION

Some years ago a man came off the street to enquire about the price of some decking and cladding. I started my sales "pitch" which started off trying to stress the need to do external decks well. He cut me short, not surprising as most retail customers seem only concerned about price and I initially thought this was the case here. But no, he explained that he was one of the paramedics attending the fatal deck collapse in Brisbane in 2009[1] and did not need to be convinced. He just wanted to be shown how to do the job well. Because of some high profile failures, decks are good illustrations of why individual joints have to be good.

 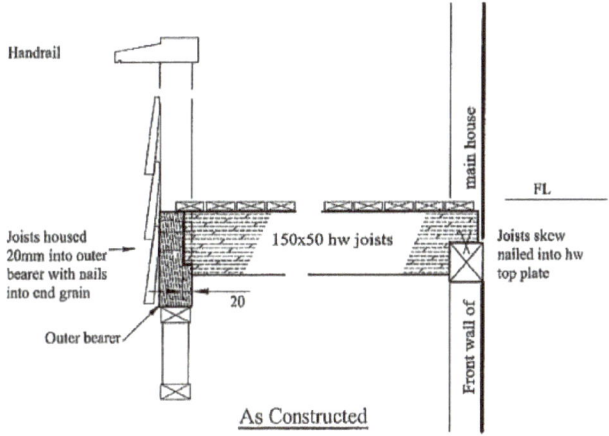

Fig. 1. Failed joint from fatal deck collapse.   **Fig. 2.** Schematic of failed joint.

A mistake was made in the construction of that covered deck ninety years earlier – yes, the timber was 90 years old. When built, the joists were cogged into the bearers and skew nailed in place. Eventually the black steel nails rusted and, for some reason, the amount of bearing of the joists into the bearer reduced over time. On the fateful day, a significant, but not an overload, event occurred and presumably the bearer bowed outwards a little. The joists unzipped and the deck dropped like a trapdoor. Builders and designers must have a mindset that spans generations when they design and construct their joints. There is no room for second-best practice. Decks do not come with a use-by date by which they should be demolished and rebuilt though, following another fatality, it could be argued that perhaps they should. Unlike the Brisbane example, a deck attached to a Yeppoon (Qld) home was only 15 years old when it deteriorated to the point it would claim the life of a seven-week-old child The Coroner advised that the decks on all rental property should be inspected after 10 years and every three years thereafter.[2]

A third deck collapse in 2013 in Lane Cove, occurred when an eight-year-old deck gave way and dropped six metres to the ground. Ten people were hospitalised, some with serious injuries, though fortunately this time there were no fatalities. The resulting enquiry showed the bearer was only attached with 12 nails! These three failures had one common thread – inspection, or lack of it, by people with

---

[1] Queensland Courts, Office of the State Coroner. *Inquest into the death of Annette Lee spencer.* URL: http://www.courts.qld.gov.au/__data/assets/pdf_file/0008/86885/cif-spencer-al-20100628.pdf Date accessed: 19 December 2016.

[2] Queensland Courts, Office of the State Coroner. *Inquest into the death of Isabella Wren Diefenbach.* URL: http://www.courts.qld.gov.au/__data/assets/pdf_file/0019/163027/cif-diefenbach-iw-20120919.pdf. Date accessed: 15 December 2016.

understanding. The surprise is not that I could find three examples but that I have only given three examples. In 2004 the building advisory service Archicentre issued a press release urging all homeowners with timber decks to have them inspected. Their concern was that decks were being built, often without any approvals and design, with inappropriate timber and poor workmanship. Their statistics indicated "approximately 6% of Australian homes have a timber balcony or deck and that about 2% of these were potentially fatal". This worked out to 8,000 life-threatening (not substandard) balconies or decks throughout the country. Despite urging a national awareness campaign through local government building departments, by 2014, Archicentre had revised the number of life-threatening decks upwards by 50% to 12,000.[3]

Fig. 3. Roof construction of a church built in 1903.

The Brisbane deck mentioned above was part of a majestic old "Queenslander".[4] These homes were not engineered but were the culmination of building practices developed for over a century as settlers attempted to understand the climate, pests and different construction materials of our "wilful lavish land" with its "droughts and flooding rain". The level of skill possessed by these builders who could draw their own plans and construct the whole homes with the only outside contractors being a plumber (and not always for the roofing) and painter is astounding by modern standards. The homes were extremely practical and liveable during a hot summer and, while the homes could be cold in winter, this was only for a short time. Joints in these houses would comprise special bolts holding the bearers to the posts, a frame that was completely mortise and tenon construction, and a nailed roof structure. Often, the only bracing was timber in the external walls. The use of bolts and strapping was minimal. Despite what could be viewed as very inadequate construction practices, it was only extreme weather events that caused failures. The church roof shown in Figure Three only failed in 2014 when the doors blew in and the roof lifted from internal pressures.

In the post World War 2 boom this style of home fell out of favour in the nationwide push to build homes that were less expensive and quicker to construct. Simplified construction practices saw a deskilling of the average builder and tasks that would be undertaken in the past by one team was now broken up into a number of trades. Timber homes evolved to the point that they were "brick veneer" (a brick skin over a timber frame with plasterboard sheeting inside) on a concrete slab. These houses achieved their goal of being relatively inexpensive to build but were flood prone and lacked the security and relative vermin free nature of the traditional design. The new style of home saw prefabricated roof trusses and metal connectors introduced but until 1974 there were not great advances in engineering that

---

[3] Willacy, Mark. Child's death increases calls for tougher standards for deck. Australian Broadcasting Commission, *7.30 Report*, April 1, 2014. URL: http://www.abc.net.au/7.30/content/2014/s3976328.htm. Date accessed: 15 December 2016.
[4] Queenslander homes comprise an underfloor of timber stumps on which is built a timber home with verandah space and sheltered edge, often only partly enclosed and a corrugated iron roof. The stumps allow for variation in ground level, and allow cross ventilation and provide protection from termite attack.

were needed.

Fig. 4. Timber homes in the aftermath of Cyclone Tracy 1974.

The need to seriously think of joints, not individually but as a totality of the structure arose following disastrous cyclones in northern Australia during the 1970's. In 1971, as a result of Cyclone Althea in Queensland there was an attempt to introduce engineering to homes to resist these recurring natural disasters. Changes were introduced but homes were still being built based largely on a now less competent builder's experience. In 1974 a severe tropical cyclone devastated the northern Australian capital of Darwin, destroying or severely damaging up to 70% of the homes in the city.[5] Much of the most damaged housing in Darwin had been engineered using the lessons learned from Cyclone Althea.[6] The catastrophe in Darwin was fundamentally a failure of the hundreds of joints not being considered as a totality in the way loads were transferred to the ground.[7] This was not always the fault of the engineering science available but could come down to selecting the wrong wind category but also because of very poor construction practices.

While Darwin was an engineering failure it was also a failure of trial and error which had prevailed till then. It was quickly realised that there were previously unknown failure mechanisms and that codes were inadequate. Cyclone Tracey required an engineering response and the shock and horror expressed in the Australian population demanded and accepted wholesale changes to timber construction.[8]

Cyclone Tracy was also a legislative failure. Till then, each state had its own and now demonstrably inadequate code. This was replaced by the nationwide *Building Act 1975* which gave legislative authority to the comprehensive provisions for the design and construction of homes and other structures called the *Building Code of Australia* (BCA). By referencing related Australian Standards they were no longer a voluntary code but had the force of law. The BCA is reviewed annually. In countries where such a rigorous design code does not exist, the BCA is immediately transferable technology and would be a very valuable tool for timber design and construction.

---

[5] National Archives of Australia *Cyclone Tracy, Darwin – Fact sheet 176*. URL http://www.naa.gov.au/collection/fact-sheets/fs176.aspx Date accessed: 29 June , 2013.
[6] Walker, George. *The Birth of the Cyclone Testing Station*. No publication details 8. This document was prepared as a contribution to the 30th anniversary celebrations of the founding of the station in November 1977. URL https://cyclonetestingstation.com.au/existing-content/public/groups/everyone/documents/advice/jcuprd-045615.pdf date accessed: 5 June 2016. Structures that needed an engineer's certificate generally fared well. Mason, Matthew and Katharine Haynes. *Adaption Lessons from Cyclone Tracy*. (Gold Coast: National Climate Change Adaption Research Facility, 2010), 36.
[7] Mason. *Adaption ...*, 36.
[8] Mason, Matthew and Katharine Haynes. *Case Study: Cyclone Tracy Final Report. U.D.* URL: http://www.riskfrontiers.com/publications/Cyclone%20Tracy%20-%20Report_FINAL.pdf Date Accessed: June 29, 2013. This report was written for The National Climate Change Adaptation Research Facility

The lesson from the Darwin cyclone was that the human toll was far too high for the same scientific approach not to be applied to homes as was given to engineered commercial structures. Very importantly, inspections by skilled professionals of the home at key stages of the construction when the joints were still visible had to be introduced. Post Cyclone Tracey timber house construction is now a mature technology and changes are likely only to be incremental.

But there is also a social aspect to joints. Since 1974 the emphasis on engineering coupled with design by professionals without the practical experience that the old contractors possessed has seen homes built that do not suit the climate. These homes may be virtually indestructible but had to be air-conditioned to be made liveable[9]. After ten years of severe drought in Queensland, severe flooding followed in 2011 and 2013 which caused serious damage to thousands of new homes. It demonstrated wisdom of the earlier style of high set construction. Modern engineered joints coupled with the practicality of the old designs make for durable and liveable home.

Fig. 5. A reproduction Queenslander style home incorporating modern engineered joints.

---

[9] In 2009 The Australian Government started the Energy Efficient Homes Package which planned to insulate the roofs of 2.6 million homes.

1. OLD AND NEW JOINTS

Our western tradition of joints requires, apart from timber obviously, tools to make an accurate joint and robust connectors to keep that joint together. Both, surprisingly have been available for a long time. It stands to reason that, without carpentry, the sedentary lifestyle associated with farming could not have been possible. When archaeologists were excavating four 7000 year old wells in Leipzig, Germany, they found timber well liners that were still in a remarkable state of preservation. After felling large oak trees with stone axes, the liners were split from them and then formed into units that were jointed with either a mortise and tenon with a timber dowel or half checked. Up to this discovery,

Fig. 6. 7000 year old well liners.

archaeologists had only uncovered the marks in the soil left by timber houses[10] so there was no knowledge of the actual joints utilised. The Leipzig discovery showed that, early on, a considerable degree of sophistication was possible in timber joints despite only having stone tools available. Saws made from serrated flint flakes set in asphalt in grooved wooden or stag horn handles have been found in Europe that are contemporary with the Leipzig well.[11]

Fig. 7. Bronze age saw from Santorini, 17th Century BC.

The impact of the wheel upon civilisation is profound but it needs to be remembered that, to first make a wheel, it took the development of metal saws and associated hand tools. Most of the hand tools we are familiar with would have been identifiable by 4000 BC and functioned well but the exception was the saw, the most vital tool needed in carpentry and the construction of joints. The earliest known Egyptian saws date back to the 3rd dynasty (roughly 4900-4700 BC). They were made from copper or bronze and had teeth without offset

and which sloped in no particular direction, making them no better than serrated knives.[12] These saws were a vast improvement on those made of flint but were laborious and inaccurate by modern standards and required finishing with an adze or rasp. A range of associated carpentry tools was also made of bronze but were applications this material was better suited to.[13] Saws of iron were known from Egypt and elsewhere but iron, at that stage in history, was not a good material for saws. It could be hardened by quenching, a process known as early as 1200 BC but this made the metal brittle. During the iron age (C. 500 BC to 50 AD) saws first had raking towards the handle which gave a cut in the pull direction only, the much weaker direction. This was necessary to stop the teeth from bending. Iron saws were so

---

[10] Wood Solutions. *Wood durability? Try 7000+ years*. URL: https://www.woodsolutions.com.au/Blog/timber-durability-7000-year-old-wood. Date accessed: 15 December 2016.
[11] Jones, P., E. N. Simons. *Story of the Saw, Spear and Jackson Limited* 1760-1960. (Manchester: Neuman Neame, 1961), 11.
[12] Jones. *Story ...*, 13.
[13] Jones. *Story ...*, 13.

inefficient that the Egyptians did not switch to them from bronze until circa 660 BC.[14] Their effectiveness increased with the development of the frame saw which avoided the bending and buckling of soft metal blades.[15]

The improvements in metallurgy under the Romans saw steel not only being more commonly available but of better quality. The impact on the ease of creating timber joints through having a more efficient saw cannot be overstated. Alongside this were improvements to the tooth design of saws which included introducing a "set" to give clearance in the saw groove to stop the saw binding. But the steel was still too soft to build a successful push saw.[17] The middle ages (476-1500) saw no real improvement in saw technology except that sawmills using reciprocating saws were operating in at least the 13th century, gradually replacing pit sawing. The change from pull to push saws probably occurred in Europe during the late 11th century through to the 12th.

What would eventually revolutionise the subject of timber joints was the invention of the circular saw (patented in the UK in 1777) where reciprocal motion was replaced with a continuous cutting action. Despite being made of cast steel, and having a low rim speed, (half of a modern saw) badly balanced, unground and with roughly punched teeth, timber production and fastening was forever changed.[18] Their immediate benefit was the production of affordable timber and would eventually speed up the production of joints through the use of power saws.

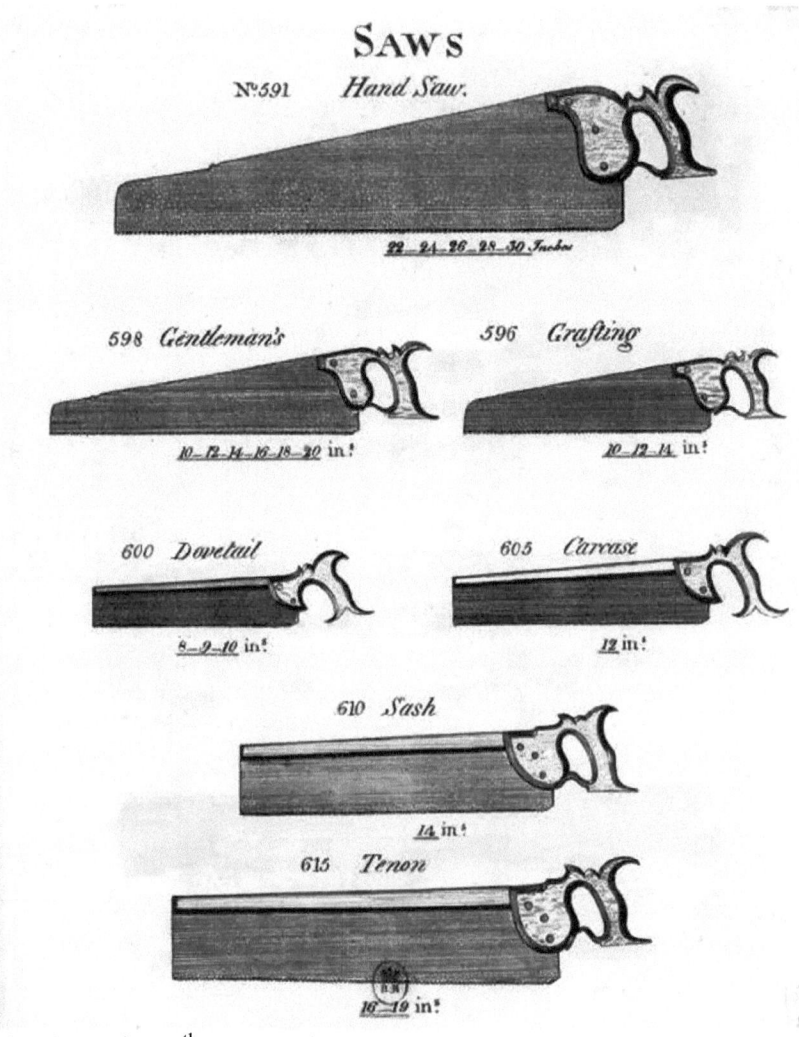

Fig. 8. Early 19th century handsaws.[16]

The industrial revolution which would enable the widespread availability of tempered steel which, in turn, gave the ability to produce efficient saws, hand, circular and band, but their very availability as such did not drive their adoption. Despite this revolution that was transforming every area of

---

[14] Jones. *Story ...*, 17.
[15] Jones. *Story ...*, 19.
[16] Smith, Joseph. *Explanation or Key to the Various Manufactures of Sheffield*. (Sheffield: Self published, 1816), pages are not numbered.
[17] Jones. *Story ...*, 17.
[18] Jones. *Story ...*, 44, 47.

manufacture, it had little effect on the British (and by default, Australian) building industry.[19] This was attributed to the British craftsman's resistance to using machinery which was an endemic feature of the 19th century industrial environment.[20] As we will see in later chapters, war and the demands of the military, in this case the Napoleonic War, would drive innovation in timber and timber joints. Timber that is so relatively inexpensive now was once a very expensive item in England which was "remarkably conservative and slow to accept sawmills. Although they were used extensively by the Dutch, French, Scandinavians, Germans and Poles, and in every new town in the British colonies of New England in the 17th century, the English consistently refused to employ them."[21] Pit saws remained commonplace in England until the 18th century and sawmills only became commonplace with the advent of steam. Sawing marine timbers by pit saw in 1811 was averaging to 4 shilling and tuppence per super foot but by mechanising it, the cost could be reduced to one shilling and four pence.[22] Smaller furniture sizes had the sawing costs slashed to one sixth.

The Institution of Engineers in the UK only defined what engineering was in its first charter in 1828 and the application of engineering based on material testing and calculation of loads on timber structures only predated this definition by a few years. Probably the most influential author and researcher was Thomas Tredgold (1788-1829), who was described as "the most influential technical author of his generation and possibly the nineteenth century"[23] and attributed by the Institute of Engineers as one of the three founders of engineering theory.[24] Being a carpenter for 11 years before becoming an engineer, he brought a deep understanding of the practical aspects of carpentry to the fledgling science. He developed (c.1820) a series of rules, called Tredgold's rules, which allowed designers to calculate member sizes that were no larger than needed, a radical new concept. They were so influential that they were being republished in various books on carpentry in the 1880's and 90's.[25]

During this period "the first commercially viable machine tooled factory system for woodworking in the world, with immense labour-saving potential" was established [26] This involved devising complex machines for processing timber into components .[27] This factory was built at Portsmouth to provide the Royal Navy's annual requirements for 130,000 blocks which required a team of 110 skilled men. Machinery designed by Sir Mark Isambard Brunel and built by Maudsley (who we will meet again in our discussion on bolts) produced the same product with 10 unskilled men saving the Admiralty £17,000 a year.[28] Generally speaking, military security around their advances in woodworking and some comprehensive patents contributed to a slower uptake of machinery but this work of Brunel's brought in a new era of woodworking that the building industry had to follow. The Woolwich Arsenal also

---

[19] Louw, Hentie. The Mechanisation of Architectural Woodwork in Britain from the Late-Eighteenth to the Early Twentieth Century, and its Practical, Social and Aesthetic Implications. Part I: The Period c.1790 to c.1860. *Construction History*, (Vol.8, 1992), 21.
[20] Louw. *Mechanisation ...*, 38.
[21] Jones. *Story ...*, 23. Pit saws were reported as being common in 1894 in England.
[22] Jones. *Story ...*, 44. These costs were determined by Sir Mark Isambard Brunel who like his son Kingdom, was a gifted engineer.
[23] Skempton, AW. *A Biographical Dictionary of Civil Engineers in Great Britain and Ireland Volume 1, 1500 to 1830.* (London: Thomas Telford. 2002), 716.
[24] Anonymous..Founder of Theory – Thomas Tredgold, Engineer *The Telegraph.* March 7, 1929, 3
[25] Newlands, James. *Carpenter and Joiner's Assistant Also A Complete Treatise on Lines.* (London: Blackie and Son. 1880), 137.
[26] Louw. *Mechanisation ...*, 24.
[27] This involved 43 different machines. It is said that :in this block machinery exist the types and examples of all modern self-acting tools, without the aid of which the various mechanical appliances of the present day could not be produced with the marvellous accuracy which has been obtained." Brunel, Isambard. *The Life of Isambard Kingdom Brunel, Civil Engineer.* (Cambridge: Cambridge University Press, 1870), 3.
[28] Louw. *Mechanisation ...*, 23.

developed and installed a steam operated planer in 1802.[29] By 1850, planers had developed to such a state that it was reported that 8 planers could do the work to a satisfactory standard of 116 men.[30]

While the building of the British Parliament House (peak construction 1845-8) had necessitated the greatest possible mechanisation and the successful tenderer was able to reduce the timber finishing by 60% over hand produced product, the real drive for mechanisation was driven by the great exhibition of 1851. It did this firstly by processing a huge amount of timber in a record time (600,000 cubic ft in one year) but by also displaying new woodworking technology to the public. There the "American woodworking machinery, although of a less stable construction, were actually superior to their British counterparts for 'boldness of design', 'ingenuity', 'simplicity', and 'fitness for the purpose', and awarded the whole Furness [an English importer of American machinery] collection a prize medal."[31] The lack of skilled workers in the US had forced mechanisation on them. The threat of foreign competition shocked the British manufacturers out of complacency[32] and they would eventually become one of the greatest manufacturers of woodworking machinery.

While this innovation was taking place at the beginning of the 19th century, light timber framing (discussed in the chapter on nails) was still some time off, as were inexpensive nails and, while screws were starting to be available, bolts were rare. Forming a joint, either by hand as had been done for millennia, or by the new accurate machinery was one thing, but how do you secure it?

What was generally utilised was a series of complex mortice and tenon and other joints and while floor joists could simply be housed into a bearer, ultimately some connections had to be made in the structure to stop the joints, particularly in the roof, from coming apart. From the earliest of times it had been possible to drill a hole, but in the absence of a bolt, what was frequently used were treenails, the term given to large wooden dowels. The success of this type of construction is well attested by the number of centuries old buildings still standing in the UK. This type of joint can still be utilised in some buildings today and appears to be making a resurgence among boutique builders.[33]

Fig. 9. Modern building using traditional heavy timber construction in the USA.

At first, wrought iron and then steel became less expensive (1870's) and it was finally possible to purchase bolts. This led to a revolution in the way that joints were constructed in the west. The timber sizes were still large but could be reduced somewhat through the improved connections but steel and bolts were still relatively expensive so they were limited and used to supplement often complex joints, refer Figures 12 and 13. Prior to the improved availability of steel and bolts, timber lengths had been limited to what could be cut from a tree but these also made possible effective joints enabling even

---

[29] Louw. *Mechanisation ...*, 26.
[30] Louw. *Mechanisation ...*, 30.
[31] Louw. *Mechanisation ...*, 43.
[32] Louw. *Mechanisation ...*, 43.
[33] They also have practical applications in very cold climates at steel can become brittle at about -30°C. One mining engineer told the author of a kit workshop constructed on a site he was working at in Alaska that was completely made of wood and secured with wooden dowels so as to avoid embrittlement of steel during the extreme winters encountered. Unfortunately, details are not available.

longer spans. What is striking from these images is the incredible skill possessed by carpenters of that vintage especially when it is considered the joints were made with very basic hand tools. It is quite possible that respect for craftsmanship led at times to unnecessary complexity in the way joints were created. Consider Figure 10 from 1866 where a simple lintel over a small window is mortice and tennoned into place and then secured with a dowel. The unnecessary complexity of this joint is in stark contrast to the simplicity and speed of construction of a modern jackstud and lintel arrangement (Figure 11) where its function has been stripped down to its barest essentials.

Fig. 10. Lintel in Gatton Railway Station built in 1866.

Fig. 11. Jackstud and lintel in modern light framing construction.

If traditional joints could be summarised it can be said:

- They were often used on large section sizes
- They were labour intensive
- They required exceptional skill
- They minimised the amount of steel and
- They were not always good (as per the Ascot deck collapse)

This book will plot the change from traditional joints to modern building practice and connection methods. There will be a total transformation in the approach to joints where now:

- They are normally used on smaller timber sizes
- They are not labour intensive
- They do not require exceptional skill
- They can maximise the amount of steel
- They must always be good.

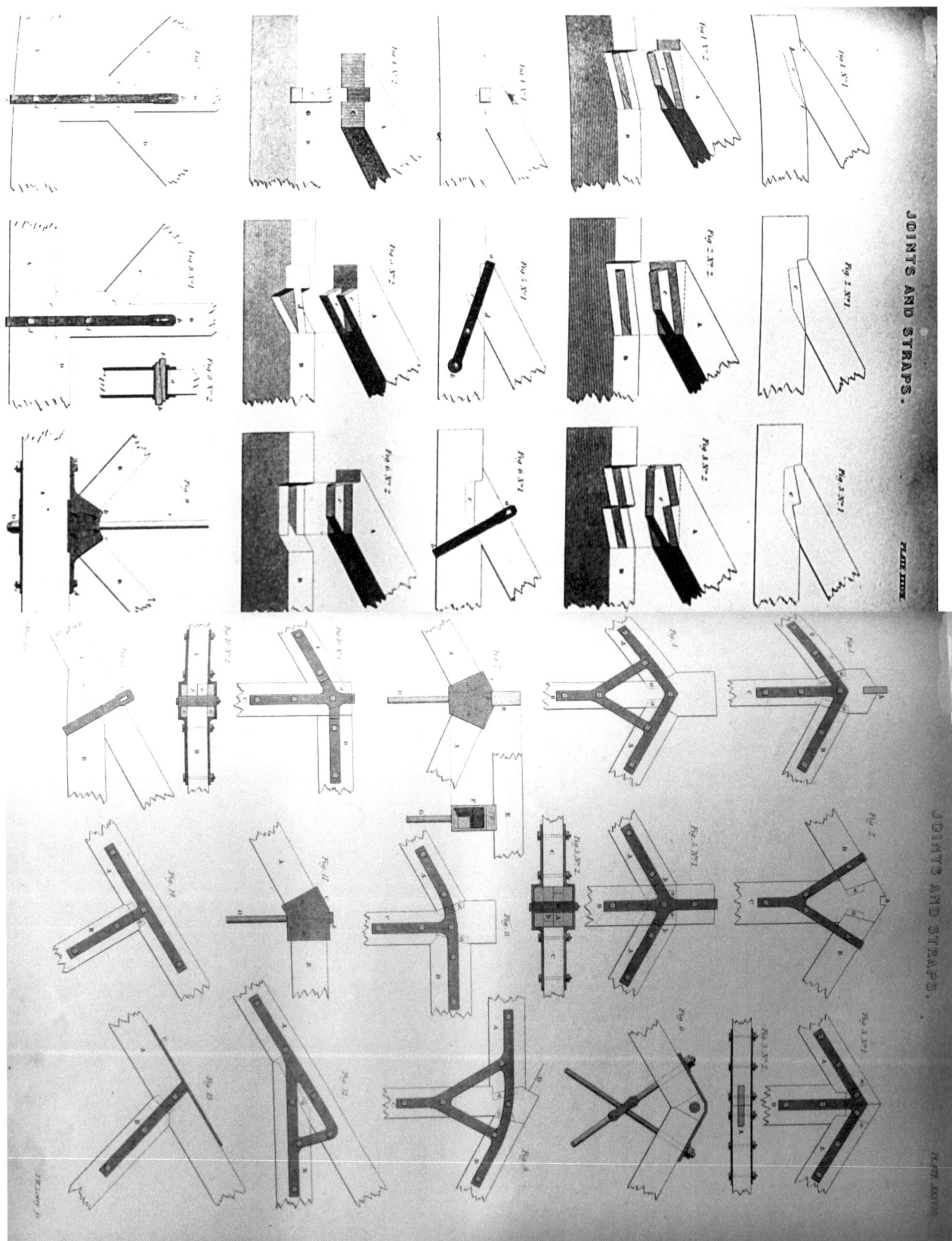

Fig. 12. British roof joints from the 1880's.[34]

---

[34] Newlands. *Carpenter…*, Plates xxxvii and xxxviii.

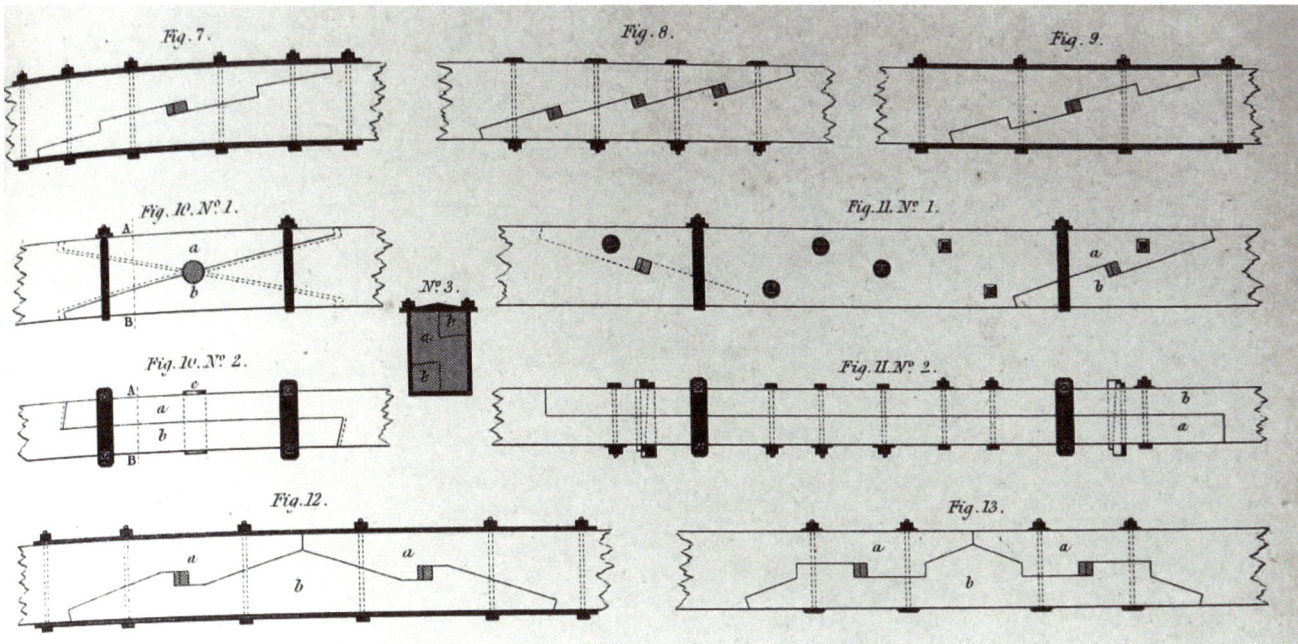

Fig. 13. British methods for joining timber to achieve longer spans in the late 1800's.[35]

While this book deals with the joints primarily from the UK (and by default Australia) and the US and the associated hardware, it is recognised that other cultures have had a rich history of joining timber that is very distinct from our own. I have spoken about high skill levels of the English carpenters but it has to be acknowledged that other societies had craftsmen probably of superior skills as the images of traditional Japanese joints shown in Figures 14 and 15 show. The final chapter of the book includes a remarkable project, the Tamedia building in Zurich, where traditional Japanese skills and design are brought together into a western multi-story building illustrating clearly that we are dealing with a subject limited only by imagination and skills.

Fig. 14. Japanese half lapped gooseneck joint sometimes used in the sole plate.

Fig. 15. Japanese double wedged locking box joint which is used in decorative corners in alcoves and some temple sole plate corners.

---

[35] Newlands. *Carpenter ...*, Plate xxxix.

Fig. 16. Bush carpentry using "Cobb and Co" wire hitches.

Many societies had far more limited access to basic tools and connections and have been forced in some cases, and chosen in others to use more "primitive" options for construction. Australia is no exception with a rich history of "bush carpentry" which used whatever was at hand. Despite its lack of finesse, it invariably resulted in buildings that stood the test of time.

Construction in bamboo, a standard method of housing construction still in many communities is an area receiving a resurgence with a number of striking examples of large architect designed structures being built over recent years. It is sobering to consider they could be built with little more than a machete and simple lashings.

Fig. 17. Traditional bamboo construction.

Fig. 18. Detail of the lashed joint.

The final chapter on timber joints will never be written as innovation, something that has been gaining in momentum over the last 150 years is not likely to diminish.

2. GALVANISED OR STAINLESS FASTENERS AND CONNECTORS

In a sealed, dry roof space or other application where the timber is not exposed to a marine environment or pollutants, the choice of bolt type is largely irrelevant. The Timberlife design life prediction software indicates that minimum corrosion will occur in galvanised bolts. This is an ideal application which historically was served well even by black steel bolts and nails where life expectancy can be measured in hundreds of years.[36] Move away from these ideal circumstances and there is a wide divergence of opinion as to when to use galvanised or stainless. Unfortunately, clear direction for additional corrosion resistance for fasteners, nailplates and strapping for different environments is not given in the BCA or The Residential Timber-framed Construction Standard, AS1684-2010 series. The Standard specifies in Clause 1.15 that "all metal used in structural timber connections shall be provided with corrosion protection appropriate for the particular conditions". With clauses like "level of corrosion protection shall take into consideration", the responsibility for choosing the correct corrosion resistance was passed to the specifier.[37] What then might these guidelines be?

When writing *Timber Preservation Guide* I asked one preservative manufacturer for their guidelines on where to use stainless and where to use galvanised bolts. They referred the matter to the lawyers in the United States who replied that we need to follow bolt manufacturers' recommendations. I then tried to find a bolt manufacturer that had a recommendation for use with treated timber and they simply did not exist. In the face of, in some cases, a deliberate omission of recommendations, to in other cases, readily available but conflicting guidelines, the correct decision of when to use stainless bolts over the less expensive galvanised can be difficult. On top of this, the specifier has to deal with customers who object to and can even aggressively oppose any cost increase that may result from nominating stainless.

Weather exposure is the complicating factor in the choice of a fastener. Should a joint be protected from the weather such as trusses in a non-ventilated roof space, the matter is quite straightforward. Correctly galvanised fasteners have proven satisfactory as the moisture content of the timber quickly drops to below 20% so decay is not an issue and as there is no ongoing wetting and drying of the timber corrosion, as will be explained, is not an issue. To come to a conclusion about which material to use externally, it is helpful to take into consideration the factors that can impact on corrosion and these are:

- pH of the timber
- The moisture content of the timber
- Preservative treatment
- Environmental considerations
- The presence of decay
- Fastener quality

---

[36] Zelinka, Samuel. Corrosion of Metals in Wood Products in *Developments in Corrosion Protection*, Editor M Aliofkhazraei (InTech, 2014), 584.

[37] Pryda. *Technical Update Corrosion Resistance of Pryda Products* Feb. 2012, 1. URL: http://www.pryda.com.au/wp-content/uploads/2016/05/Post-Anchor-Guide-March-2012.pdf. Date accessed: 15 December 2016.

Species	pH	Trouble
Blackbutt	3.6	yes
Mountain ash	4.7	no
Ironbark, red narrow leaf	4.0	yes
Spotted gum	4.5	no
Rose gum	5.1	no
Jarrah	3.3	yes
Radiata	4.8	no

Table 1. Corrosion from acidity of timber.[38]

If the joint is to be exposed to any moisture, the acidity of the timber has to be considered. Corrosion can be an issue when the Ph drops below 4.3. While the pH of a piece of timber varies within the piece and from piece to piece there are published values which can be used as a guide (Refer Table One). If the specification is just, say, "F14" it has to be assumed that a species with a lower pH will be supplied. By nominating a species outside of the problem range, such as spotted gum, the consequences of corrosion can be minimised.

Given the relatively benign chemistry of wood it can appear a simple environment where corrosion is not a challenge but wood "has a complex interaction with water that greatly affects its physical and chemical properties including corrosion."[39] Wood is a hydrophilic material meaning it has a strong affinity with water and some species can absorb up to 200% of their dry mass as water. This water can be either free liquid water or water vapour in the cells and cavities or bound water held by intermolecular forces in the cell walls. The point where the free water is expelled and only bound water is present is called the fibre saturation point and is normally about 30% moisture content. In service, moisture is given off and taken in freely until it reaches equilibrium with its environment.[40] Below a moisture content of 15-18% embedded fasteners do not corrode but will start to increase around 20% and reach a maximum corrosion rate at or above fibre saturation point.[41] The implications are that there are applications for fasteners that present no challenge from timber moisture such as roof trusses made from kiln dried pine and others which are very difficult such as a pergola in a tropical region which is being continually wet.

Another factor that impacts upon corrosion when fasteners are weather exposed is the preservative used. Newer preservatives ACQ and Tanalith E (also called copper azole or CuAz) have proven effective replacements for CCA as far as timber decay is concerned. But without the chrome and arsenic, these alternative chemicals require a significantly higher level of copper in the timber than with CCA. A higher concentration of water soluble copper is "more likely to initiate serious corrosion of susceptible metallic components embedded in or in contact with these timbers".[42] Corrosion could be from four to nine times that of CCA over a one year period.[43] The iron and hydroxyl ions released from the

---

[38] This table is drawn from Bootle, Keith R. *Wood in Australia, Types, properties and uses, Second Edition*. (North Ryde: McGraw Hill Australia, 2005), 60-1 and Table 2.3.3 of Forests and Wood Products Australia. *Manual 6 – Embedded corrosion of fasteners in exposed timber structures*. (Melbourne. Forest and Wood Products Australia: 2007). On this scale a pH of 0 is highly acidic, 7 is neutral and 14 is highly alkaline. The scale is logarithmic with a 10 fold jump between each unit.

[39] Zelinka. *Corrosion ...*, 568.

[40] Zelinka. *Corrosion ...*, 568.

[41] Zelinka. *Corrosion ...*, 574.

[42] Li, Z.W., N.J. Marston and M.S. Jones. *Corrosion of Fasteners in Treated Timber* Study Report SR241 2011 (Branz, 2011), i

[43] Li. *Corrosion ...*, i. Bootle initially corrosion was thought to more than double that of CCA. *Wood ...*, 62. Simpson Strong-Tie after testing 2600 samples assessed them as a little more than double. Anon, *Preservative Treated Wood Technical Bulletin No. T-PRWOOD08-R* (Pleasanton: Simpson Strong-Tie,. 2008), 3. This assessment was based on accelerated weathering tests based on the American Wood-Preservers Association Standard E12-94 *Standard Method for Determining Corrosion of Metal in Contact with Treated Wood*.

corrosion attacks the cellulose components of the timber causing "nail sickness" whereby there is significant loss in the structural integrity of the joint.[44] By contrast, it has been argued that the chrome and/or arsenic of CCA can have a passivating effect on fasteners.[45]

Fig. 19. Sons of Gwalia headrig.

A further factor that will influence the choice of fasteners is the climate. The Australian climate is very varied, from hot humid tropics to dry deserts. The heritage listed headrig from the Sons of Gwalia mine at Gwalia (a two hour drive north of Kalgoorlie) in Western Australia in the Great Victoria Desert was built during 1886-8 from 300x300 Oregon pine. About a third has been replaced with kauri which is not a great deal more durable (In Ground Durability 3) but basically the timber has lasted ten times longer than you would normally expect. The bolts are just black steel without any corrosion protection and they, just like the timber, have survived because there is seldom any moisture. Invariably, designers will have to deal with the effects of a more aggressive environment.

The embedded corrosion hazard zone map in Figure 20 shows Australia broken up into three zones. These zones are determined by the mean annual surface equilibrium moisture content ($SEMC_{mean}$). The boundaries for these are C the highest risk 15%, B a medium risk at 12% and A, the lowest and where Gwalia is found, 9%. To this climate map the designer has to factor into his assessment the impact of marine exposure (less than 1 km from the coast) and, further, whether the products being joined are sheltered from the rain, and if not, is it a vertical or a horizontal surface.[47] This means there is a large variation in risk due to environmental considerations alone.

Fig. 20. Embedded corrosion hazard zone map.[46]

---

[44] Li. *Corrosion ...*, ii.
[45] Rammer, Douglas, Samuel Zelinka, Philip Line. *Fastener Corrosion: Testing, Research and Design Considerations* a paper given at World Conference on Timber Engineering 2006, 1.
[46] FWPA. *Manual 6 ...*, 7
[47] FWPA. *Manual 6 ...*, 6-8

Fig. 21. Different performance between galvanised fastener and bracket.

The galvanising process is far from novel as it was first patented in 1837 and its effectiveness was recognised to such an the extent that by as early as 1850 the British galvanising industry was using 10,000 tonne of zinc a year to protect steel. But what is not often appreciated is the difference between atmospheric corrosion of galvanised fasteners as we would see in, say, a steel bridge and corrosion of the same fasteners in timber. Because the coating works well in the one application it was assumed that it will perform equally well in others and this has not proven to be a safe assumption.[48] In the case of atmospheric corrosion of zinc, specific oxides form (hydrozincite and smithsonite) on the surface and protect the zinc from further corrosion. When installed in timber, different oxides form (namuwite, simonkolleite and sometimes hydrozincite) which do not give the protection layer seen with atmospheric corrosion. Without this passivating layer, wood corrosion on galvanised fasteners can even be faster than non galvanised steel fasteners.[49] To complicate matters, under different exposure conditions galvanised fasteners have been shown to corrode more slowly than steel.[50]

A further factor to consider when choosing galvanised or stainless is the deteriorating quality of many if not most imported galvanised bolts. Careful specification of the bolt coating thickness, while important, is ultimately meaningless if it is not backed up regular testing of grade compliance.[51] At the time of writing there has started to be some regulatory awareness of this problem as corrosion has been reported in hold down bolts in houses, an application which is sheltered from the weather.

But before discussing this, consider first a well made and well galvanised bolt. It is important to understand that even this bolt does not have the same longevity as galvanised steel rod of the same thickness. Bolts are galvanised in small batches in wire cages which are then spun at high revolutions to remove excess zinc and give a clean thread. The typical minimum coating thickness for a 10 mm bolt or larger would be 390 g/m^2 or 55 microns. By contrast, the minimum coated thickness for steel over 6 mm, which sits in the vat for up to 10 minutes is 600 g/m^2 or 85 microns and regularly reaches 700-900 g/m^2. Longevity is dependent on the zinc coating so normal steel could have an expected life of 30 to 50% longer than that of the bolt.[52] But that is assuming that the bolt is of high quality and that does not necessary follow. Now that cup head and general use hexagon head bolts being imported to Australia, the life expectancy of the galvanised finish has deteriorated dramatically.

---

[48] Zelinka. *Corrosion ...*, 587.
[49] Zelinka. *Corrosion ...*, 574-5. See also Zelinka, Samuel, Rebecca Sichel, Donald Stone. Exposure testing of fasteners in preservative treated wood: Galvimetric corrosion rates and corrosion product analysis in *Corrosion Science* 52 (2010) 3947 where it is reported that several researchers have observed that zinc corrosion protected products can corrode more rapidly.
[50] Zelinka. *Exposure ...*, 3947.
[51] I am aware that ITW Proline do this but smaller importers may not.
[52] Robinson, John. *Specifiers Manual.* (Carole Park: Industrial Galvanisers, 2013), 15.

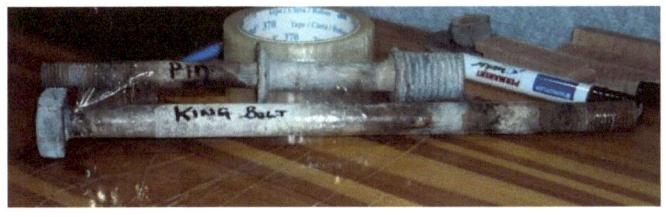

Fig. 22. Australian made galvanised bolt after 50 years service in Millmerran, Qld. Bolts were removed in 2001.

Fig. 23. Imported galvanised bolt after 12 months in Gatton, Qld c. 2003.

While poor performance of many galvanised fasteners is known among the industry, trying to find information in the public arena on the seriousness of the situation is very difficult. It is almost like a conspiracy of silence. The one article I could find based on tests conducted on four batches of bolts purchased from different manufacturers in China summarised the situation as follows "The anti-corrosion performance of the four hot-dip galvanizing bolts obtained from different companies were all unsatisfactory. The causes of the above phenomenon are the lower thickness of the hot-dip coating, too much defects on the surface of the coatings and the elemental composition impurity".[53] How great was the variability of the galvanising? The average coating thickness on individual bolts went from 130 micron[54] to 34 microns and the minimum was 13 microns which happened to be on the same bolt that averaged 130 microns. This is greater variability than timber and can mean that the bolt, not the timber, is the weak link in the system. Note that Industrial Galvanisers indicate that a well galvanised bolt should be 55 microns.

It is further helpful to consider manufacturers' and industry body recommendations. The Timber Preservers Association of Australia (TPAA) has a very simple recommendation for fasteners in CCA – "Hot dipped galvanised nails, bolts and coach screws should be used in corrosive environments, e.g. swimming pool structures, marine structures, [and] in the immediate vicinity of the sea-coast, where airborne salt spray represents a very severe hazard to metal fittings and fixings".[55] This is not in keeping with one of their members, Arch Chemicals, recommendations. I view the TPAA guidelines as far from adequate and can lead to premature failure.[56]

There is no recommendation at the time of writing by TPAA for non-chrome, non-arsenic treatments. Two very useful guides for the Australian specifier are published by Timber Queensland and, as mentioned, Arch Chemicals. Arch Chemicals' publication for the Americas, Corrosion and Hardware Recommendations for Treated Wood[57], is the document used as the basis for

---

[53] Li. Cuoxin, Shanjing Xia, Yilang Peng. Anti-Corrosion Performance of Four Hot Dip Galvanising Bolts in *Applied Mechanics and Materials Vols. 395-396* (2013), 708-71.
[54] The paper was expressed in um, there is one micron to one um.
[55] Timber Preservers Association of Australia *Fasteners in CCA Treated Timber*. URL: http://www.tpaa.com.au/fastenerscca.htm. Date accessed: 25 March 2012.
[56] I am aware of a boardwalk in the Cairns region where galvanized bolts were used on the seafront and bolt replacement started after only six months.
[57] Arch Wood Protection, Inc. and Arch Treatment Technologies, Inc. *Hardware Recommendations for Treated Wood*. June 6, 2006. (No publication details), 2-3.

recommendations by that company for Australia. It is reproduced in simplified form which removes information only relevant to North America.

Recommendations for Copper Azole and CCA Treated Wood[1]					
Important Note: In severe environments having an unusually high corrosion hazard such as those that are continuously wet or within 5 miles (8 km) of salt water, in critical architectural applications where appearance is of great importance, and in structural applications of an especially critical nature or where an exceptionally long service life is required, the use of hardware having corrosion durability equivalent to or greater than 304 or 316 stainless steel should be used					
	Indoors always Dry (<15% MC)	Protected from weather Dampness OK	Outdoor in Weather - regular wetting	Coastal applications	Wood foundation & other critical applications
Fasteners	Mild Steel, EP*(2)*, HDG, MG, Copper, 304/316 SS	HDG, MG, Copper, 304/316 SS	HDG, MG, Copper, 304/316 SS	304/316 SS	304/316 SS
Connectors, light gauge steel	HDG *(3)*, Copper 304/316 SS	HDG, 304/316 SS	HDG, 304/316 SS	304/316 SS	NA
Connectors, heavy duty welded steel	HDG, 304/316 SS	HDG, 304/316 SS	HDG, 304/316 SS	304/316 SS	NA
Flashing *(4)*	Copper, 304/316 SS HDG *(3)*	Copper, 304/316 SS HDG	Copper, 304/316 SS HDG	304/316 SS	Copper, 304/316 SS
Table 2. Corrosion protection with Copper Azole, and CCA.					

Borates & Dricon® Fire Retardant Treated Wood[1]		
	Indoors Always Dry (<15% MC)	Protected Can be damp for extended periods
Fasteners	Mild Steel, EP, HDG, MG, Aluminium, Copper, 304/316 SS	HDG, Aluminium, Copper, 304/316 SS
Connectors light gauge steel	EP, HDG, MG 304/316 SS	HDG. 304/316 SS
Connectors Heavy duty welded steel	HDG, MG 304/316 SS	HDG -ASTM A123 304/316 SS
Flashing	HDG, MG, Aluminum, Copper, 304/316 SS	HDG, MG, Aluminum, Copper, 304/316 SS

Table 3. Corrosion protection with Borates and Fire retardant treatments.

Notes to Tables:

(1) Key to Metals in Tables: HDG: Hot-dipped galvanised steel MG: Mechanically galvanized steel EP – Electroplated SS: Stainless Steel

(2) Arch regards the use of hot-dipped galvanised fasteners as preferable to using non-galvanised or electroplated steel nails, though these are regarded as acceptable when attaching framing to copper azole treated timbers if that wood has been dried after treatment and will remain dry in a H2 application. Their recommendations point out, but do not take issue with, the International Residential Code which allows non galvanised bolts when the diameter is ½" (12mm) and larger, even for foundation bolts. We would question the wisdom of this.

(3) Standard galvanised strapping is regarded as acceptable for fastening copper azole treated wood to foundations providing it is used in a H2 application.

(4) Aluminum in the presence of moisture is subject to dissimilar metal corrosion when in contact with either CCA or copper azole treated wood. "Aluminum should only be used in normally dry applications

where a barrier can be installed that

(a) provides complete separation of the aluminum (without penetrating fasteners) from the treated wood and that,

(b) will remain intact for the service life of the flashing. Aluminum nails, screws, fasteners and connectors should not be used in wood treated with copper based preservatives".[58]

As far as fasteners with ACQ are concerned, I was not able to find thorough recommendations similar to those that were available from Arch for their CCA alternatives. Koppers Performance Chemicals urge "compliance with building codes for the intended use" which, as has been shown, is very vague. Fastener recommendations for use with CCA [similarly for ACQ] products include hot dipped galvanised, stainless steel and other fasteners as recommended by the fastener manufacturer."[59] They also advise not using ACQ preserved wood in direct contact with aluminium. Considering the serious implications that can follow a fastener failure due to the effect of treatment, the difficulty with these recommendations are that "manufacturer's recommendations" simply are not readily available, if at all.[60] I am loathe to say it, but there seems little option other than to follow the guidelines of their competitor. As an order of non chrome, non arsenic treated timber is likely to contain either ACQ or Tanalith E, regardless of what is specified, it would have been useful to know if ACQ had extra corrosion resistance requirements to Tanalith E. Timber treated with ACQ is more corrosive than timber treated with Tanalith E.[61]

Fig. 24. Z275 bracket used near a swimming pool.

The different nailplate manufacturers came to an agreed position on where to use stainless and where to use galvanised connectors in 2016. This is reflected in Timber Queensland's *Technical Data Sheet 35, Corrosion Resistance of Metal Connectors*. This guide identifies different corrosion zones:

- Sea spray zone (less than 1 km from a surf coast, 100 m from bayside areas)
- Coastal zone (1 – 10 km from surf coast, or 1 km from bayside)
- Industrial zone (close to complexes emitting corrosive gasses)

---

[58] Arch. *Fastener...*, 4.
[59] Koppers Performance Chemicals. *Naturwood ACQ*. 2006, 2. URL: http://www.kopperspc.com.au/pdf/micropro-brochure.pdf. Date accessed: 15 December 2016, and Koppers Performance Chemicals. *Lifewood CCA*. 2006, 2. URL: http://www.kopperspc.com.au/pdf/Lifewood-cca-brochure.pdf. date accessed: 15 December 2016.
[60] Dr Saman Fernando, Manager, Engineering Research Development and Innovation for Ajax Engineered Fasteners advised that Ajax did not have recommendations. *Pers. Com.* March 27, 2012.
[61] In all cases, the ACQ H3.2 [corrosion] values ... were approximately 1.5 to 3.8 times that measured for the CCA H3.2 timber ... and CuAz H3.2. Kear, G, Hai-Zhen Wu, Mark Jones. The *Corrosion of Metallic Fasteners in Untreated, CCA-, CuAz-, and ACQ-based timbers. Branz Study Report* 153. (Judgeford: Branz, 2006), 92.

- Special Hazard (e.g. enclosed swimming pools where stainless may even corrode and beyond the scope of the data sheet)
- Low hazard zone (anywhere outside the four areas listed above)

This is then broken down into three exposure conditions

- Enclosed (within a closed roof, floor and wall cavity)
- Sheltered (subject to wind-blown salt but not washed with rain, e.g. open garages and sub-floors)
- Exposed (experiencing both weather and rain, e.g. decks and pergolas).

In all exposed allocations in the four areas covered by the guide, 316 grade stainless is required (or else specially prepared plates). For the sheltered applications, an area not differentiated by some recommendations prior to 2016, a standard Z275 (275 grammes of galvanising per m2 total both sides i.e. 138 gsm actual per side) can only be used in the Low Hazard Zone, other applications require either stainless (Seaspray Zone) or the addition of soft seal paint (Coastal and Industrial). Where there is little risk of corrosion such as in an enclosed and sealed roof area Z275 can be used even in a Seaspray Zone. Further, these recommendations are for non treated timber and those treated with waterborne preservatives can require additional paint protection which for simplicity basically forces you to stainless.[62]

Further driving a specifier to stainless at least with the thin connectors is the difficulty in achieving 600 gsm thickness of galvanising unless the plates are abrasive blasted and more reactive steel is used.[63] There is also the danger that if 600 gsm is achieved that the coating may be brittle. Another consideration is the short design life of Soft Seal of only up to two years.[64] Advice received from the Galvanisers Association of Australia to the author differs slightly from that of Timber Queensland and generally does away with the difference between sheltered and exposed applications. Their recommendation is included as Appendix 1.

The recommendations differ from those of Arch as the Timber Queensland guidelines recognise different risks within the marine environment breaking it up into different risk categories and locations within the building. The Arch guidelines also do not differentiate between a coastal area that has sea spray and a sheltered bayside. But when the extra care needed to make the plate suitable for treated timber is factored in they are probably little different in practice. Note that in the case of Pryda, the recommendations apply to the whole range of their products, not just nailplates and include post supports. In effect, 316 stainless or equal is recommended for all external applications.

---

[62] We used to use nailplates in our bridges painted with micaceous iron oxide. The process involved purchasing the plates, sending them to a galvaniser who pickled them to remove the Z275 coating, hot dipped them and then had them shipped them back. We then had to send them off to a paintshop and then wait for them to be shipped back. There was a long lead time and it was very expensive but also very effective.

[63] McLean, Will. *Pers. Com.* 2 December 2016. Will is Market Development Engineer at the Galvanisers Association of Australia. Specifying the steel will beyond most specifiers.

[64] CRC Industries (Aust) Pty. Limited. *Technical Data Sheet Product No. 3013,3014, 3015,3016.* URL: http://www.crcindustries.com.au/assets/files/tds/softseal-3013-tds.pdf. Date accessed: 15 December 2016.

Fig. 25. Test Structure for long term exposure by BRANZ in New Zealand

Finally, consideration has to be given to actual durability trials. The extent of corrosion in fasteners in ACQ and Tanalith E treated timber has generally been assessed by accelerated testing, not through independent inspection of real life or quasi-realistic applications.[65] The conclusion of long term exposure trials conducted by BRANZ concluded in 2011, was that "it was impossible to correlate the corrosion of metal in timber exposed to a high temperature and humidity environment to the corrosion rate under real service conditions".[66] The study went on to conclude that incorrect interpretation of the different accelerated tests has led to incorrect material election and structural design.[67]

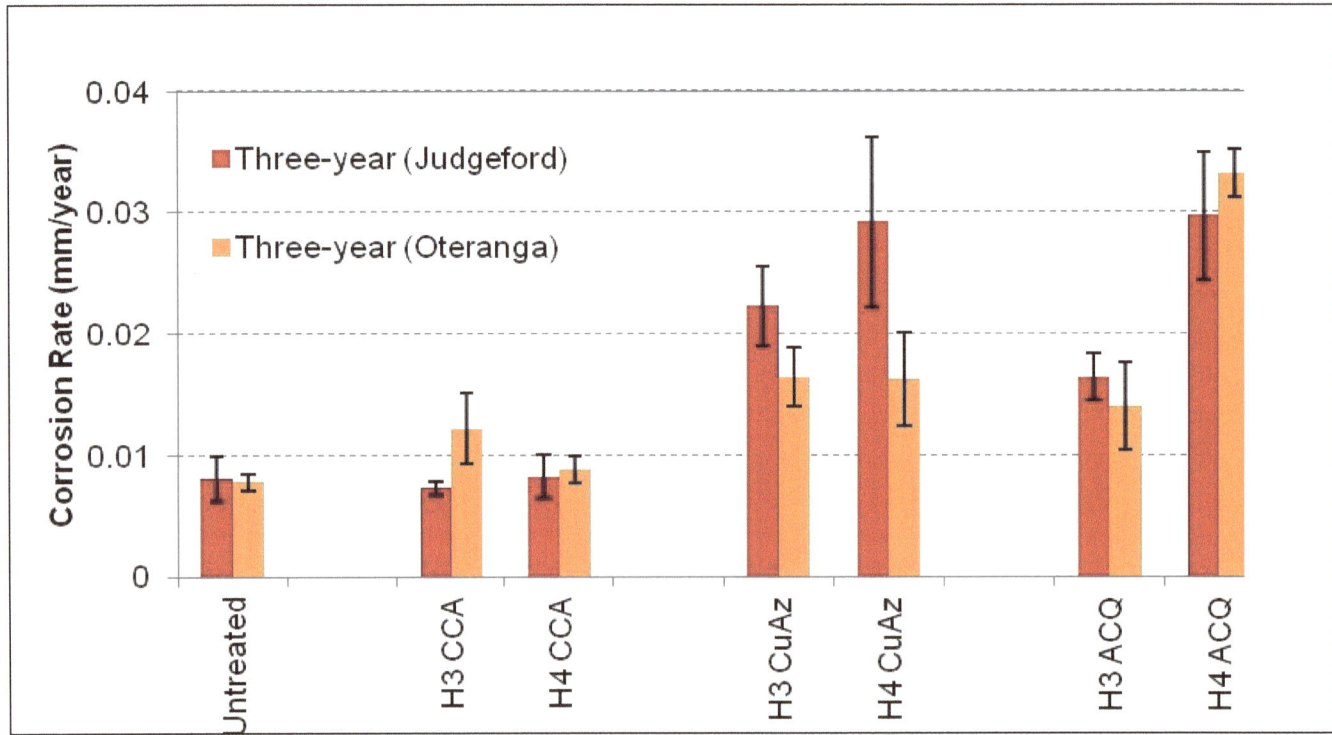

Fig. 26. Corrosion rates of hot dipped galvanised nails after three years of exposure in New Zealand. The orange bar is at Oteranga Bay (sea-spray zone) and the red bar is 5 km from a sheltered tidal estuary with hills in-between at Judgeford.

---

[65] Li. *Corrosion ...*, 6.
[66] Li. *Corrosion ...*, 5. These trials were conducted at two sites, one very close to breaking surf and the other five km from a sheltered tidal estuary and protected by hills. These are both areas where manufacturers recommend stainless fasteners but galvanised are frequently used.
[67] Li. *Corrosion...*, 5.

While the chemicals present in the CCA formula are thought to provide passivation effects to the steel, the new chemicals do not contain such inhibitors.[68] Long term testing was undertaken by BRANZ in a relatively benign sheltered marine application, (5 km from an estuary) and in a sea spray zone. The results showed increased early corrosion rates in H4 ACQ of 3.5 times that of H4 CCA in mild steel and at least 7.4 times with fasteners with zinc coatings. That corrosion slowed in time but, after 3 years, the figures were 1.4-1.9 times for mild steel and 3.1-3.6 for zinc. While corrosion of the heads was more closest to the sea, embedded corrosion at the site close to breaking surf was only a little higher and in some cases the shafts had more corrosion in the sheltered area.

Among their findings were that:

- mechanically plated screws did not work with any preservative containing copper[69]
- The corrosion behaviour of zinc coated fasteners should be of great concern as, "if the timber gets wet, it is doubtful that hot dip galvanised nails and mechanically-plated screws will be able to meet the durability requirements of the NZBC and relevant New Zealand Codes"[70]
- The sound condition of the head did not necessarily reflect the condition of the shaft[71]
- Stainless performed well without obvious signs of corrosion.[72] Either 316 or 304 should be used as a "sensible interim precaution"[73] to reach the 50 year durability requirement
- A lot more work has to be done on researching fasteners under different environments to find out what the long term (>15 years) effects of corrosion are.[74]

The trials also showed that generally speaking, corrosion severity is as follows: Untreated - CCA - Tanalith E - ACQ[75] which is in same order from low to high of the copper present in the timber. As ACQ and Tanalith E are difficult if not impossible to tell apart and usually specified side by side it is necessary to assume the worst case for corrosion.

Finally, there is one other factor to consider and that is the ductility of the fastener, particularly hardened screws, a factor unrelated to corrosion issues listed above. When these screws are used to fasten timber to steel these screws are prone to snapping and for this reason the major Australian manufacturers will not certify their screws in this application. The hardening process causes the screw to lose its ductility but timber movement, particularly with hardwood, requires that the fastener be ductile. Nails are ductile but the timber movement causes them to come out in decking applications. Conversely, the screw will not come out but, because of its loss of ductility, can snap. One manufacturer reported that this is more of a problem in areas "more than 100 km from the coast as we see greater variance of moisture content with rain and then extremes of dry."[76] Stainless is now all but universally recommended by manufacturers for use as decking screws into steel.

---

[68] Li. *Corrosion...*, 1.
[69] Li. *Corrosion...*, 65.
[70] Li. *Corrosion...*, 66.
[71] Li. *Corrosion...*, ii.
[72] Li. *Corrosion...*, 65.
[73] Li. *Corrosion...*, 66.
[74] Li. *Corrosion...*, 66.
[75] Kear. *Corrosion...*, 11.
[76] Kuhn, Herb. *Pers. Com.* September 13, 2016. Herb is Managing Director, Simpson Strong-tie Australia.

To bring this matter to a conclusion I will quote a considered opinion of one of my readers; "it is my firm belief that galvanised fasteners are only suitable for timber constructions if the conditions are and continue to be ideal. Due the unpredictability and number of variables that influence exposure conditions as well as the substrate, selecting more corrosion resistant fasteners significantly reduces the risk of premature corrosion."[77]

An Australian aspect to Choosing Decking Fasteners.

Areas of Australia can have climates so severe in their range of wet and dry, hot and cold that it is more extreme than selected test areas for fasteners in the United States. This brings in an Australian aspect to fastener choice. Herb Kuhn, Managing Director of Simpson Strong-Tie advised that in their "experience areas like North East Victoria and the High Country are the most extreme and as you get further from the coast the humidity variation is most extreme. West of the Great Divide is the other area that is a real challenge for us, again due to the hot and dry summer and then if there is large amounts of rain in the winter or wet seasons, this creates the challenging environment that we need to deal with."[78]

It was further stated that while "Corrosion performance is definitely one consideration and proximity to swimming pools and the ocean should automatically direct us to use stainless steel as opposed to plated steel screws. However ductility should be of equal consideration if we are looking for a long lasting deck structure. A hardwood deck that is fully exposed to the rain and direct sun will expand with the rain and shrink with the dry, it will dry out without humidity and swell with it and all of this creates movement of the decking boards. Keeping the decking well oiled will reduce the affect that these conditions have on the timber, however the use of stainless steel screws has a significant benefit in ensuring that the fastener does not break with the movement of the decking."[79]

Bushfire is also an Australian consideration and in bushfire prone zones steel joists are often used to support Timber decking and special bi-metal screws have been developed where a carbon steel drill point, wings and the first four threads are welded onto a fastener that is otherwise stainless. This gives the ductility that is needed while at the same time allows the steel joists to be drilled.

---

[77] Duyvestyn, Oscar. *Pers. Com*. June 30, 2016. Oscar is Principal Consultant – Coatings & Advanced Materials with AECOM.
[78] *Pers. Com*. November 11, 2016.
[79] Kuhn, Herb. *Pers. Com.* November 11, 2016.

Alternatives to Stainless Steel Bolts

Is there an alternative to stainless steel? Quite possibly, and that is ITW Proline's Tech-Shield™ coated bolts. ITW is the only Australian organisation I am aware of (at the time of writing) which has taken the issue of poor performance of imported galvanised bolts very seriously. At the time of writing this is the only such product on the market in Australia. These bolts have an epoxy coating applied with an electric charge which ensures an even coating. In conjunction with ITW technical coating specialists in Asia and the United States, they developed a new advanced barrier coating that helps bolts protect from the chemicals found in treated timber. This ultimately extends the life of the bolt. When tested at an Independent laboratory to international and Australian standards Tech-Shield™ provided, on average, 3.9 times the protection of their regular hot dipped galvanised bolts when used in treated pine. Unfortunately, they were not available when I operated my business so I don't have personal experience. Specifiers should check with the manufacturer to determine the suitability of this product for their application.

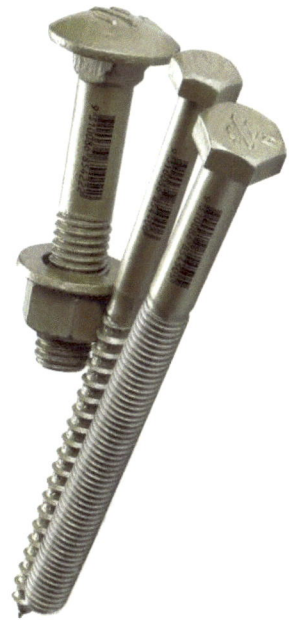

Fig. 27. Bolts with corrosion resistant paint.

3. NAILS

The ubiquitous nail, cheap and plentiful, is a very underrated fastener. Clearly the capacity of a nailed joint is limited by its comparatively small surface area and low withdrawal resistance. This downside can be overcome by using gussets and increasing the number of nails as well as changing the geometry of the nail and adding adhesives to the shank. The case history at the end of this chapter will show that even standard nails can be used to build durable and economical timber structures spanning almost 52 metres.

With alternative fasteners such as screws and glues and alternative building methods now available, the overall sales of nails in Australia has been decreasing[80] but they still remain very sizable. No other fastener can match it for ease of fabrication and the nailed joint, the mainstay of normal timber constriction exploits this to the full. The true value of the nail, not its cost, is best appreciated when it is not available. One of our colonial pioneers wrote "December 14th [1836] The last fortnight has been devoted to the building of my hut, which nearly adjoins the tent, and is 12 feet wide by 21 feet long. Only six nails were used in its construction; the uprights, crosspieces, beams and joists being all tied together with cordage."[81] There is also the record of the Tahitian maidens selling their virtue for a nail.[82] The now everyday abundance of nails should not obscure us to the fact that the nail, made from wire as we know it, is a relatively modern item.

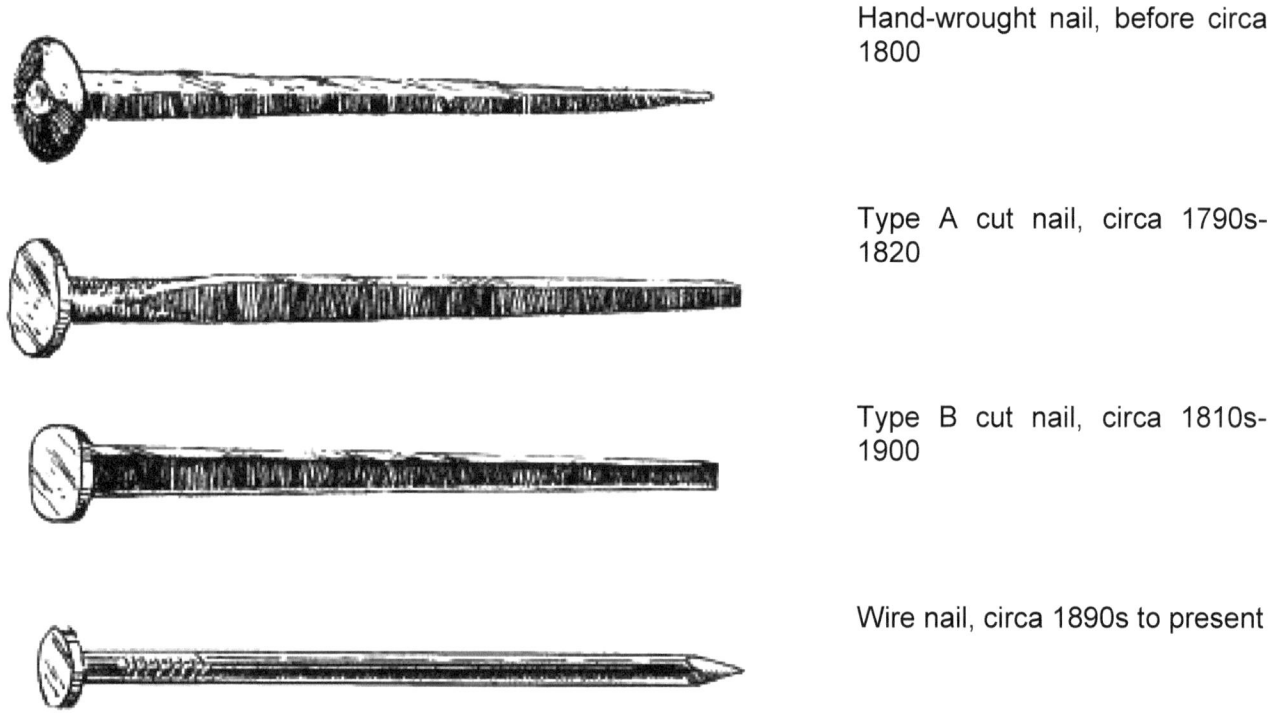

Fig. 28. Development of the nail.

---

[80] Goode, Andrew quoted in *The Secret History of Nails* by Ray Sparvell. URL: http://www.domain.com.au/news/the-secret-history-of-nails-20160829-gr3b9p/ Date accessed: 21 October 2016.
[81] Gouger, Robert. Memoranda of a Residence in Holdfast Bay in Penelope Hop, Editor. *The Voyage of the Africane*. (South Yarra: Heinemann Educational Australia, 1968), 126.
[82] Cook, James. *Captain Cook's Journal*, Tuesday 6th 1769. URL: https://ebooks.adelaide.edu.au/c/cook/james/c77j/-chapter3.html. Date accessed: 20 October 2016.

Nails, of course, have been known for as long as man has been working metals. Bronze nails, used to attach wooden planks to ship frames have been recovered from ancient shipwrecks. Copper alloy nails have been found dating back to before 3000 BC in Egypt. Their cost must have been substantial as the famed 43.6m long funerary ship of Khufu, about 4,600 years old was built entirely without nails. The bronze age ended c.1200 BC when it was replaced with iron the ores of which were much more common. This meant iron could be produced at a lower cost than bronze but it was initially a soft spongy material filled with slag.

Fig. 29. Bronze ship nail 1st century BC -3rd century AD. Length 135 mm, width 2-7 mm and head 18 mm © University of Queensland

After processes had been developed by the Hittites c 1500 BC to remove the impurities and after hammering into a solid mass it became useful.[83] The widespread use of nails would be governed by the reduction in cost of mining and processing. Romans mining practices and production of processed metal would rarely be matched until the industrial revolution. In 1957, at one archaeological site, Inchtuthil in Perthshire Scotland, a former roman fortress, about 7 tonne (about 900,000 items) of nails were discovered.[84] While steel was known for millennia, the iron that was produced in quantity was not steel but wrought iron.

Before the wide availability of steel, wrought iron[85], or worked iron as the word means, was the most common form of malleable iron. Wrought iron has very low carbon content but has fibrous glass like slag inclusions – up to 2% by weight which gives it a grain similar to timber. The two materials are in physical association, as opposed to an alloy as found in steel. The product was refined by hammering it when it was white hot, hence its name but even after this working its constitution remained very variable. Wrought iron is very malleable and ideal for "clenching", where nails protrude through the items being fixed and are folded over. Wrought iron reached its peak of production in the 1860's

The shape of nails had not changed from ancient times right through to the Tudor period, and being hand made with basic blacksmith tools from iron nail rods, there was not a great deal of room for change. While these nails with their tapered square shafts, the pattern for five thousand years looked primitive to our eyes, their holding power could be greater than a new wire nail. The four edges "as sharp as knife blades, these edgy nails – ancient hand-wrought as well as the machine cut ones of the 1800s – sliced the wood's fibres along the length of the tapered shank so that when the wood swelled with even the slightest dampness, the nail was bound into the wood with great strength."[86] Nails were made in great quantities during the Medieval period and sold by the hundred in a great range of sizes and shapes. Nails were classified by their price per 100 items from the 1400's[87] and were still referred to that way in a machine manufacturer's brochure of 1888 and even much later.[88]

---

[83] Newton, David. *Chemistry of New Materials.* (New York: Facts on File Inc, 2007), 4.

[84] McConchie, Matasha. *Five iron nails from the Roman hoard at Inchtuthil* (ANU. UD),. 3. URL: http://slll.anu.edu.au/sites/slll.anu.edu.au/files/default_images/McConchie_Classics_Occasional_Paper_1.pdf. Date accessed: 17 October 2016.

[85] The present use of the term to describe welded mild steel ornamental work can lead to disappointment when old ironwork is being restored.

[86] LeFever, Gregory. Cut Iron Nails in *Early American Life.* (Firelands Media Group June 2008), 60,

[87] Nelson, Lee. Technical Leaflet 48, Nail Chronology as an Aid to Dating Old Buildings in *History News*, Volume 24, No 11 (November 1968). pages not numbered (History News is the journal of the American Association for State and Local History)

[88] Nelson. *Nail ...*, pages not numbered. The terminology soon bore no relation to actual cost

Mechanisation of the blacksmith's art started to occur in the 1600's which included rolling and slitting mills to make nail rods[89] though the actual nails themselves were still made one at a time. The radical shift in nail making came with the change from wrought nails to cut nails, Most of the innovation came from the United States with 88 patents issued between 1791 and 1815, indicating the importance of low cost production of nails. Various machines, operated first by hand, then water and later steam made nails from iron bars. The cross section of the bar was the thickness and length of the nail and the bar itself was about 3.6m long. The shank taper was made by wiggling the bar from side to side (or flipping) by hand, producing the Type A cut nail in Figure 28 above. The heads were initially formed individually by hand but the process soon became mechanised. This type of nail continued until about 1820. Whereas the smallest nail in the Roman hoard at Inchtuthil was thought to take 45 seconds each to make once the bar was heated, one machine dating from 1789 was producing 120,000 nails in a week![90]

Wrought nails continued to be made for several decades after the introduction of less expensive cut nails as they were superior in some applications, especially those requiring clenching.[91] Whereas the wrought nail had the grain running length wise, the grain in the cut nail was crosswise. More effective nail cutting machines were developed by the 1810's whereby the bar was flipped between each stroke which, in turn, was sheared off in a cutter set at an angle. With the nails all aligned in the same direction mechanisation of the heading of the nail was practical. This is represented by the Type B (Figure 28) cut nail that was made in quantity till about 1900 and are still produced. Cut nails can be used in the US for fastening flooring and other specialised applications. These were the first truly uniform nail.

The ready availability of nails led to a revolution in timber construction in the US. Before their wide availability, most construction used a heavy timber frame system similar to barn construction using four and six inch (100 and 150 mm) square members. The elaborate mortise and tenon joints employed required skilled carpenters. This would change in the 1830s, when articles were published in the US "about a revolutionary new framing system, called "balloon framing" by later builders. This system called for standard 2x4 lumber, nailed together to form a sturdy, light skeleton. Builders were initially reluctant to adopt the new technology, however, by the 1880s, some form of 2x4 framing was standard'.[92] In Australia by 1870 this style of construction became commonplace but Australian practice differed from American as extensive use of carpentry joints was still employed, including mortising the studs into the plates.[93]

The need for wide sheets of iron for steam engine boilers drove the development of large rollers driven by reliable steam engines. Previously these wide plates had to be made by beating thick plates under a water driven helve hammer. Grain inline cut nails also needed wide sheets that could be sheared across the grain. The first plant producing wide sheet was established in England in 1803 and were common enough by 1830 to be applied to improved in-line grained nails.[94] This produced a nail with four sharp corners and a flat point.

---

[89] Wells, Tom. Nail Chronology: the use of Technically Derived Features in *Historical Archaeology* 1998, 32(2) 81.
[90] Nelson. *Nail ...*, pages not numbered.
[91] Nelson. *Nail ...*, pages not numbered.
[92] Indiana Department of Natural Resources. *Historic Building Research Handbook.* (No publication details) 1. URL: http://www.in.gov/dnr/historic/files/records_search_handbook.pdf. Date accessed: 21 October 2016
[93] Bell, Peter. Continuity in Australian Timber Domestic Building: An Early Cottage in Burra in *Australian Historical Archaeology* 8, (1990): 8. URL: http://www.asha.org.au/pdf/australasian_historical_archaeology/08_04_Bell.pdf. Date accessed: 23 October 2016.
[94] Wells. *Nail ...*, 85.

Fig. 30. Wafios N6 nail making machine.[95] **Fig. 31.** A coil of nail wire.

Wire is made by drawing a rod through a number of ever reducing holes until the required diameter was achieved. Apart from the power changing from humans to water through to steam, the process itself was little changed from mediaeval times to the middle of the 19th century. While the grain was in line, iron wire was not considered suitable for nails as, firstly, plate for cut nails could be produced more cheaply and secondly, the narrow un-tapered sides of the soft iron could not be driven into hardwood without pre drilling.[96] Machinery for making wire nails was first developed in England, France and Germany with the first US factories being established in the 1850's. These machines could produce a completed item, point and head without any manual stages. Originally these machines made small size nails such as for making cigar boxes but, when the machinery was perfected in the 1860's to 70's, nails large enough for building construction started to be made.[97] Large scale steel production began in the late 1870's with the adoption of a modified Bessemer process which involved melting pig iron (the intermediate product of iron smelting) and blowing oxygen through it. The widespread adoption of wire nails followed once the cost of steel was less than wrought iron. In 1886, only 10% of nails in the United States were made of soft steel wire but within six years they had overtaken cut nails and by 1913, 90% of the production was wire nails.[98]

Thirteen types of steel nails are covered under AS 233-1980 (reconfirmed 2015) indicating how sophisticated the design and production of hand nails has become, tailoring the needs of the fastener to the application through small changes to the design. Cold drawn (also known as hard drawn) low

---

[95] "These machines having been engineered and made in Germany were extremely reliable – some of our machines were close 50 years old and still running without issue when we decommissioned them." Goode, Andrew. *Pers. Com.* 21 October 2016. They produce 350 nails a minute.
[96] Wells. *Nail ...*, 86.
[97] Nelson. *Nail ...*, pages not numbered.
[98] Visser, Thomas. *Nails: Clues to a Building's History.* University of Vermont, Historic Preservation Research. URL: http://www.uvm.edu/~histpres/203/nails.html. Date accessed; 21 October 2016.

carbon steel is used which has sufficient ductility to bend 90 degrees at its midpoint without cracking at a radius equal to the diameter of the nail. There is no provision for stainless or other materials. The minimum tensile strength varies from 750 MPa for the thinnest nail (1-1.6 mm) down to 400 MPa for 8-9.5 mm spikes. There is provision for lower strength nails to be supplied on agreement of the two parties.[99] From the roughly hewn nails of the blacksmith, nails are now produced within very fine tolerances for diameter (ranging from .03 mm for the finest nail up to .08 mm for the decking spike) and length (1 mm to 3.0 mm).[100] These fine tolerances are necessary as the "tooling can possibly be damaged if the wire diameter is under the low end of the tolerance but the other major factor is that the grippers that pull the wire into machine are not able to grip the wire properly resulting in inconsistent nail lengths".[101]

Australia once had a healthy nail manufacturing industry but now it has virtually all moved overseas apart from some specialty fasteners. Most nails now sold in Australia come from China. Soft imported nails, once a problem when imports first hit the market are generally a thing of the past.[102] While most major brands of imported nails follow Australian standards there can be variations in designs to suit particular applications [103] and there is provision in the standard to vary this on agreement.[104]

Fig. 32. Howard Hughes' "Spruce Goose", the construction of which led to the development of the nail gun.

This ability to produce large quantities of nails within fine tolerances has given rise to the myriad of collated gun nails. The actual invention of the nailing gun is attributed to Morris Pynoos, an aeronautical engineer, to assist with the construction of Howard Hughes' "Spruce Goose" which was started during World War 2. The wooden fuselage was nailed together and glued and the nails then removed.[105] A commercially available nailing gun was reported on in the March 1950 edition of Popular Mechanics. It weighed 32 pounds (14.5 kg) and could drive 40 to 50 nails a minute. The gun was used for floor sheeting and used when standing. Interestingly, the nails taken in its magazine are described as 7,8 and 10-penny nails.[106]

Nail guns and the nails they drive have come a long way since being introduced to the trade in 1950. The nails can be collated in paper, plastic or wire in strips and coils and the guns, now much lighter, can be driven by pneumatics or electricity and even be cordless, powered by propane. The nails are not made to Australian Standards but are designed for specific applications. The nails themselves can be

---

[99] Standards Australia. *AS 2334-1980 Steel nails – Metric series*. (Sydney: Standards Australia, 2015) 4.2.
[100] Standards *AS2334 ...*, 5.1-5.3.2.
[101] Goode, Andrew. *Pers. Com.* 12 December 2016.
[102] .Goode, Andrew. *Pers. Com.* 21 October 2016.
[103] Goode, Andrew. *Pers. Com.* 12 December 2016.
[104] Standards *AS2334 ...*, 5.2.
[105] Oliver, Myrna. *M. Pynoos, 84 Civic Booster, Engineer* in Los Angeles Times July 10, 2002 (obituary).
[106] Popular Mechanics . Nailing Machine Speeds Building. (Chicago. Popular Mechanics March 1950) 96.

very sophisticated, such as twisted or ring shank, domed head, stainless decking nails with adhesive coatings and are constantly used in place of traditional hand nailing. Despite this sophistication and undoubted speed and ease of use, the effectiveness of gun nails in certain applications has been questioned.

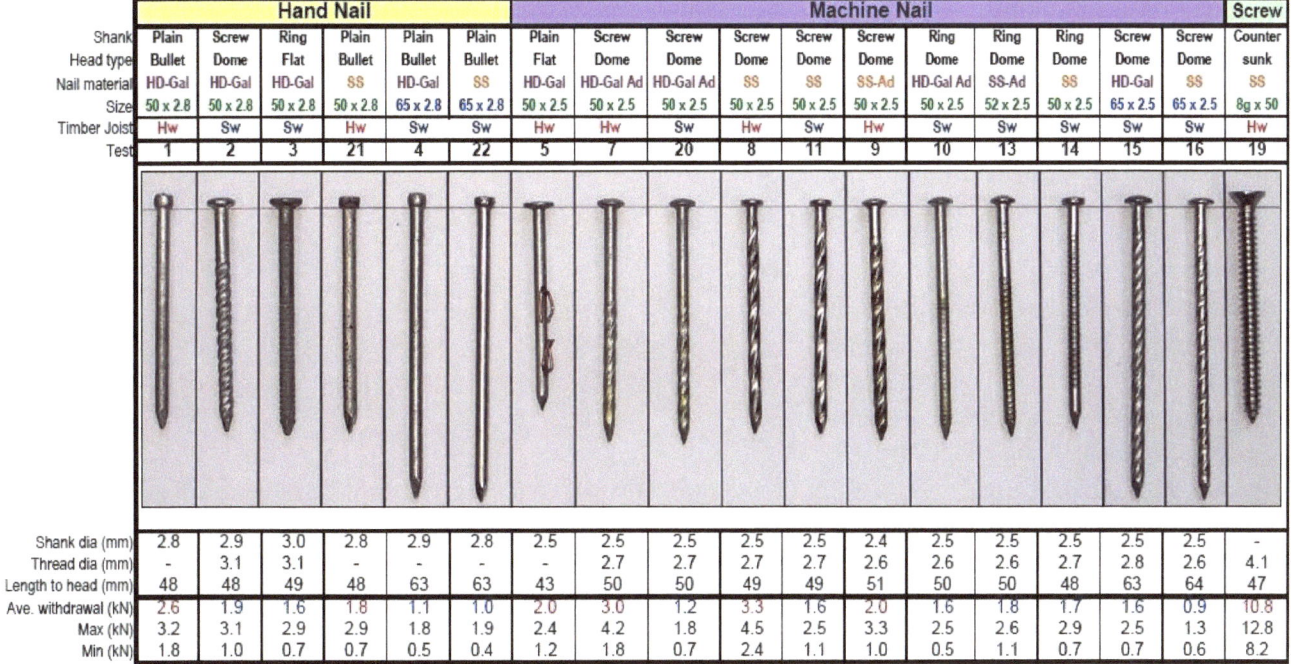

Fig. 33. Deck nail withdrawal tests.[107]

Testing was undertaken by Timber Queensland in 2005 where a number of gun nails were compared to the standard arrangement of two 50 mm hot dipped galvanised nails for securing decking. They concluded, echoing a well known advertising slogan for the time "NAILS AINT NAILS" saying "The withdrawal capacity and hence deck 'holding power' of nails is very much related to the nail geometry design (roughness and profile of shank, nail diameter etc) and the variability of the nails performance in the timber." The report advised "Published recommended nailing specifications may need to be amended to refer to specific nails and requirements placed on nail suppliers to provide 3rd party verified withdrawal capacities."[108] In the discussion on timber connectors it will be shown that the inappropriate use of gun nailing has led to them being banned in that application in Queensland. Another area that has been highlighted where inappropriate use of a nailing gun has caused issues is in the US for the installation of felt and timber roofing shingles.

---

[107] Haywood D, C. Mackenzie. *Deck Nail Withdrawal Tests FWPRDC project 02.1209.* (No publication details or page numbering) Table 3.
[108] Haywood. *Deck ...,* pages not numbered.

An entirely appropriate and very successful use of gun nail is end nailing studs through the top and bottom plate. While there is little resistance to withdrawal when nailing into end grain, this is not an issue as, in a completed assembly with a comprehensive system of hold downs from roof to slab, there in no likelihood of withdrawal.

The choice to hand nail or gun nail has been put this way: "As the use of power equipment increases ... quality of workmanship has also entered into the picture. Pneumatic nail guns and screw guns have appeared, adding speed at the expense of (according to many) quality. A contractor's selection of the appropriate fastening method remains a choice based not only on strength, but also on value and workmanship."[109]

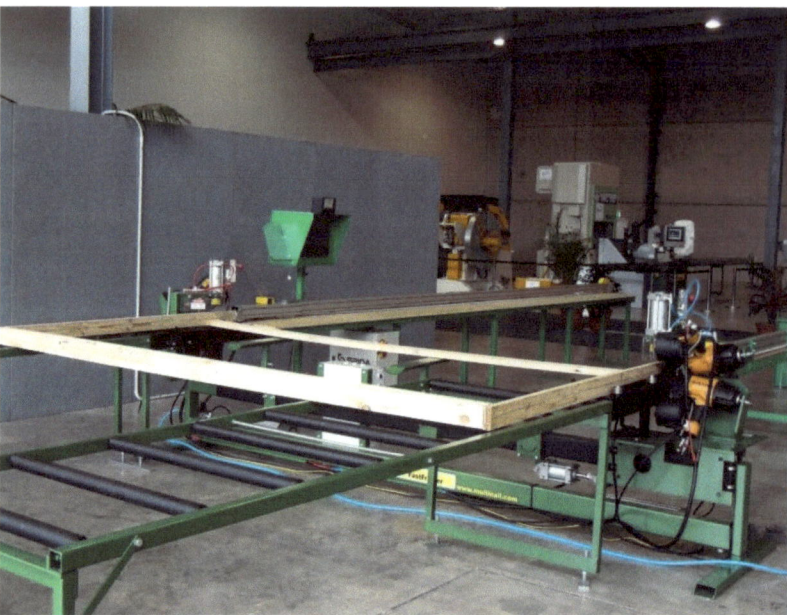

Fig. 34. End nailing studs on framing table.

Spacings on nails

Because the diameter of nails are so much smaller than bolts the actual distance between the nails is not large and often just a little common sense can see this achieved without any particular knowledge of the requirements of AS1720.1 Timber Structures Code. The required spacings are given in Table Four.

Spacing Location	Code Requirement D = Nail Diameter	e.g. 3.05 mm dia. nail
End Distance	20D	20 x 3.05 = 61 mm
Edge Distance	5D	5 x 3.05 = 15 mm
Between nails along grain	20D	20 x 3.05 = 61 mm
Between nails across grain	10D	10 x 3.05 = 31 mm
Table 4. Minimum Nail Spacings[110]		

---

[109] Sauter, David. *Landscape Construction, 3rd Edition.* (Delmar: Cenage Learning, 2011), 90.
[110] Standards Australia. *AS1720.1 – 2010 Timber Structures Part 1 Design measures,* (Sydney: Standards Australia. 2010), Table 4.4.

It is impossible to meet these requirements in certain applications such as nailing 90 mm decking on to 50 mm joists. The spacing with a 2.8 mm nail will be about 45 mm when it should be at least 56 mm which is why it is very common to see the floor joists split (Figure 35) and then potentially decay. Once the joist is split the nails can start to withdraw. In this case a staggered alignment (always a good practice), maintaining a suitable edge gap and driving the nails in at an angle, protects the joist from splitting.

Case study – Aircraft hangars from World War 2.

Fig. 35. Joist split along the grain as the nails are too close.

Fig. 36 House carpenters nailing igloo truss.

Fig. 37. Framed igloo almost ready for sheeting.

World War 2 forced changes to timber construction that would have otherwise been slow in coming, if coming at all. As one author wrote, "The war removed every major factor that had restricted design and construction in timber in this country during the preceding two decades. It severely curtailed steel supply for building. A single agency co-ordinated timber supply [the Controller of Timber]. Timber design technology and experience became available (from the Americans as well as from local professionals). Most importantly, an urgent demand existed for large structures. As a result, largely untried timber technologies became the foundation of most major building construction in Australia for more than three years. From its establishment in 1942 until its dissolution in February 1945, the AWC [Allied Works Council] built thousands of structures all over Australia. Many of them were in timber."[111] Borne out of emergency, they featured a new aesthetic in timber that was lean, strong and graceful.[112]

One of the most conspicuous reminders of this period in many communities was the aircraft and stores buildings known as "igloos" built from three pinned nailed box arches. They were built in large numbers some of which are still standing despite their temporary nature and liberties taken with engineering.[113] Their designer was the French engineer Emile Brizay, a refugee who fled Singapore, before its fall, for Australia.

---

[111] Nolan, Gregory. *The Forgotten Long span Timber Structures of Australia*. A Thesis for the Degree of Master of Architecture, University of Tasmania, 1994. 14.
[112] Nolan, Gregory. Extraordinary Buildings - Wartime design ingenuity with wood in *timber +DESIGN* Autumn 2008.
[113] A working stress for the timber was adopted which was 33% larger than recommended by the CSIR. Nolan. *Forgotten ...*, 14.

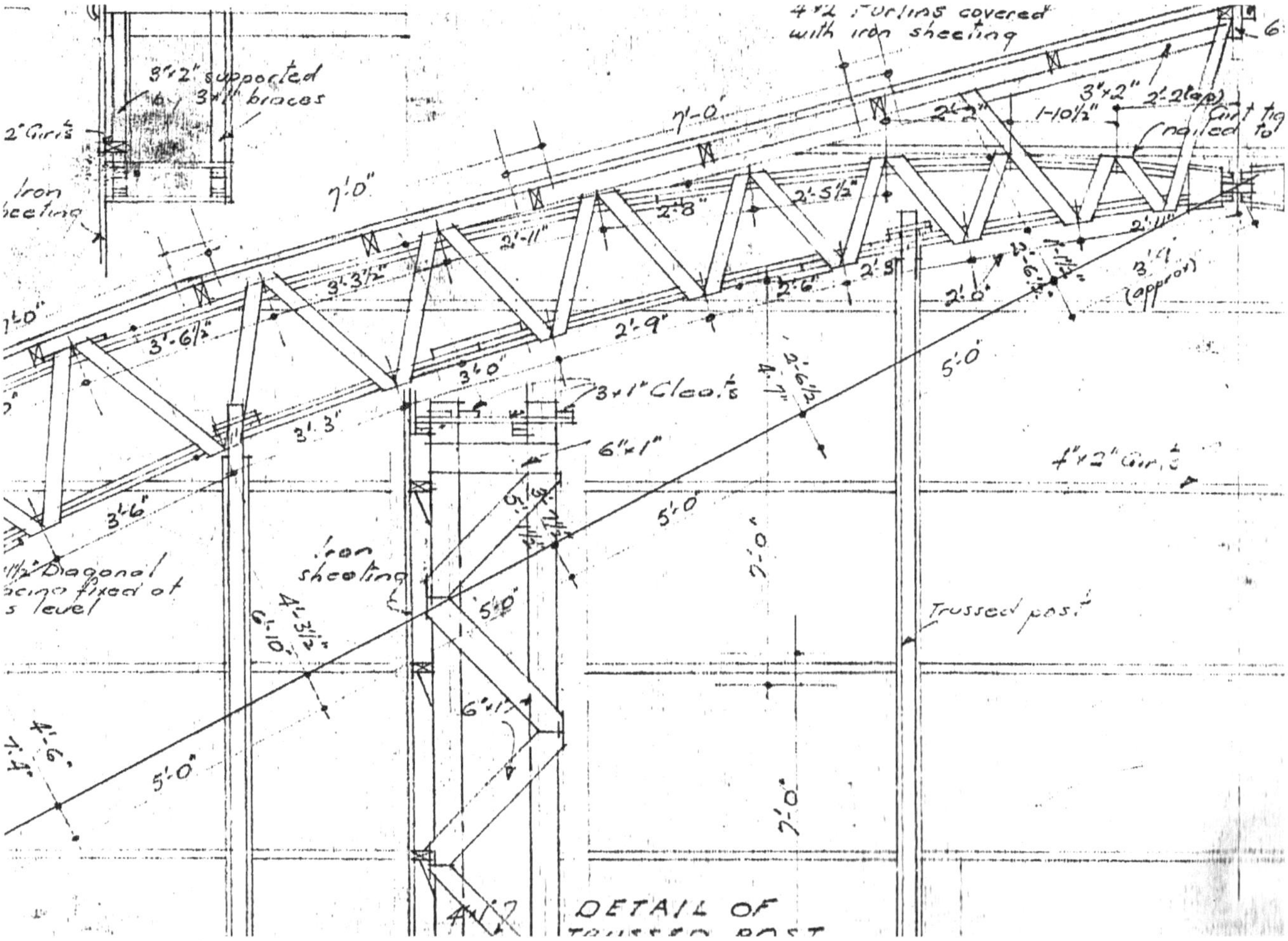

Fig. 38. Detail from US igloo design constructed at Townsville.

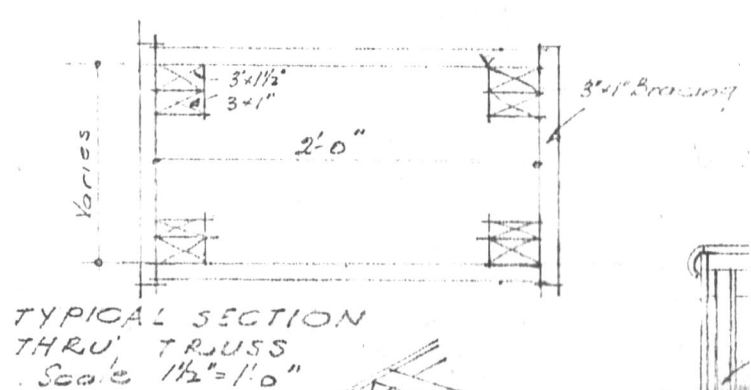

Fig. 39. Section through box truss of US design of 104 ft igloo.

There were variations in the design between the American and Australian versions. Igloos initially started off as 104 ft (31.7 m) spans intended to carry camouflage netting. Protecting planes on the ground was critical in the early stage of the war when Japan had air superiority. The igloos were soon modified to take a corrugated fibro or iron roof. The Australian design for the 104 ft building used 4x2 inch (100x50 mm) for the main cords. The timber cord members for the American 104 ft igloo trusses (Figure 39) were laminated from 3x1 ½ inch (75x38 mm) and 3x1 inch (75x25 mm) for the main arch cords and the diagonals varied between 2x1 inch (50x25 mm) and 4x1 inch (100x25 mm). Later designs reached 170 ft (51.8 m). No examples of lighter American version of the 170 ft igloo survive but several examples of the Australian version exist and their main cord was 5x2 ½ inch (125x 63 mm) and the braces are 3x1 ½ inch (75x38 mm). The box arches for both spans were completely nailed construction. The examples that still exist in Archerfield are 356 ft long (108.5 m) and, in 1994, were the longest clear span timber structures in Australia.[114]

These buildings were very successful and Brig. Gen. Hugh Casey, the Chief Engineer of the Southwest Pacific Area reported to the US that "it uses small commercial size lumber, much of it of scrap size and can be readily constructed and erected at low cost with relatively small expenditure of time and materials."[115] He recommended the design for widespread application. An Igloo 104 ft wide, 200 ft long and 25ft high, without a concrete floor but with an iron roof and timber end walls could be built in nine days by 30 experienced men. After the war, Australian designers soon forgot what was achieved with timber and reverted to steel.

A Family Memory

During World War 2, my father served in the Civil Construction Corps and was foreman in charge of the rebuilding of Amberley air base near Ipswich. He had an apprentice who wrote to the apprenticeship board and complained that despite being an apprentice builder all he was doing was making concrete formwork for "sheds". Representatives of the board turned up at Amberley and had words with my father about this. He blew his whistle, stopped work and had all the gangs sit around in a circle, each in their own gang and introduced them to the man from the Apprenticeship Board. He asked them in turn where they came from and why they were at Amberley. And the answer was the same from each crew. They had come from all around Australia for the honour of working on these igloos. The technology was far beyond anything they had ever seen in Australia before and told how they had to be trained in its implementation by US engineers. My father then explained how the success of the structure was dependant on the accurate placement of the concrete abutment at the end of the arch. The apprentice was given the most responsible position of any of the workers on site. Nothing more was said.

---

[114] Nolan *forgotten* ..., 20.
[115] Casey, Hugh. *Igloo Type Construction for warehouses, Hangars and Aircraft Hideouts As Developed In Southwest Pacific Area*. This document is a report to the Chief of Engineers, Unites States Army October 21, 1942. Document reference AG 634(10/21/42)E.

4. THREADED FASTENERS

Possibly the one thing driving the competitiveness of timber structures against alternatives is the efficiency and low cost of modern connectors. Normally it requires so little skill or knowledge of design to fasten timber to timber that handymen routinely use nails, bolts and screws to construct all manner of timber structures. The rapid proliferation in the use and complexity of threaded fasteners which has seen their everyday application in light framing is a relatively recent development occurring only over the last 150 years. Screws particularly are being seen as a natural alternative to nails because of their adaption to specialist applications and very low price.

The screw, an inclined plane wrapped around a centre pole, is one of the six "simple machines" for multiplying force as described during the Renaissance.[116] For something so deceptively simple as a threaded fastener, it still took 2000 years to perfect The origin of the thread can be traced back before Archimedes (c. 287-212 BC) whose name was given to the water screw. The origins of the screw could be at least 350 years earlier to at least the Assyrians who are thought by some to have used it to water the hanging gardens of Babylon.[117] The water screw was used from ancient times to drain bilge from ships and dewater mines. Some attribute the first studies into and development of the screw to achieve motion to Archytas of Tarentum (c. 420-350 BC), the last and greatest of the Pythagoreans and known as the founder of scientific mechanics. This type of screw would be used in wine and olive oil presses. But it is a big leap from the water screw and wine press to our modern threaded fasteners. Yet without this leap our modern world would have been impossible. Without the ability to produce a precision threaded fastener, quick and efficient fastening of timber where nails would not suffice would have been impossible. Further, the myriad of precision tools which form part of any modern construction, timber or otherwise, also would have been impossible.

Joining Timber with Screws

The Romans certainly understood the principle behind the screw and used it in industrial[118] and military applications and it was also found in medical implements which were recovered from Pompeii after its destruction. They probably invented the first screws for going into wood. These screws were bronze or silver and the threads were made by filing or by soldering on a spiral wound wire.[119] Their holding power of the mechanical bond was much greater than a nail which was only held by friction. Unfortunately, their cost and complexity worked against the widespread use of screws and the knowledge of wood screws was lost with the fall of the Roman Empire.

Virtually every tool in a carpenter's box has an ancient predecessor but not the screwdriver, or turnscrew[120] as it was originally termed. This tool is so revolutionary that the case has been made for it to be described as the best tool developed in the last millennium.[121] One of the oldest known written reference to a screwdriver is in 1723 in France as the *tournevis* and it probably is a French invention but an illustration from 1588 shows a slotted screw requiring, obviously, a screwdriver.[122] Screws are

---

[116] The other five are the lever, wheel and axle, pulley, inclined plane and wedge.
[117] Strabo *Geography* XVI.1.5.
[118] Ulrich, Roger. *Roman Woodworking.* (New Haven: Yale University Press. 2007), 59.
[119] Kruszelnicki, Karl. Nuts and Bolts – Part 1. URL: http://www.abc.net.au/science/k2/trek/4wd/nuts1.htm Date accessed: 2 November 2016.
[120] And still called such in the 1870 catalogue of William Marples & Sons.
[121] Rybczynski, Witold. *One Good Turn, A Natural History of the Screwdriver and the Screw.* (New York Scribner 2000), 13-44.
[122] Found in Augustino Ramelli's *Le diverse et artificiose machine* where in a drawing of a flour mill, a screw is illustrated partially installed and showing the thread. Witold. *Turn ...,* 51.

known earlier where they were used to secure the lock to firearms. Screws were still rare but the tendency to use threaded fasteners gained momentum with their use in items such as clocks and armour. Very little happened in thread innovation until the 15th century but Leonardo Da Vinci designs for screw cutting machines in the late 1400's appear to have been overlooked. A screw industry did not develop till the mid 18th century where a cottage industry arose where threads were formed in forged blanks by filing or using a crude lathe. The threads were imperfect and the thread shallow.[123]

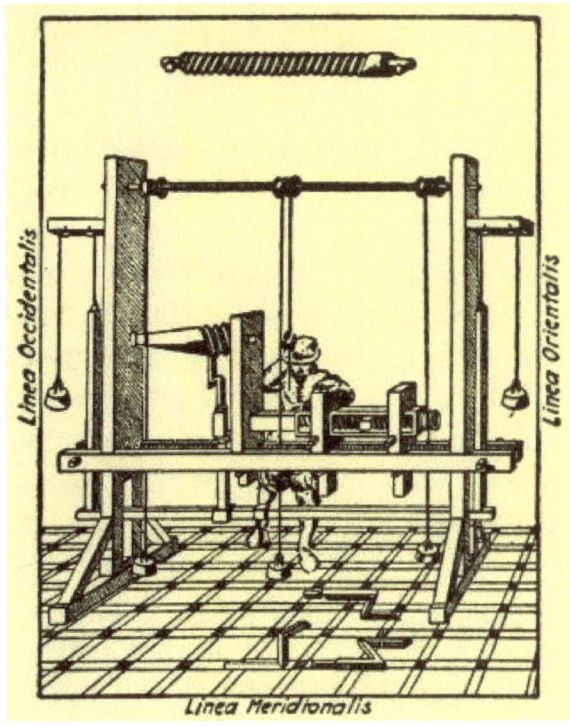

Fig. 40. Besson's Screw cutting lathe.

Probably the first machine for making screws, but in timber, was made in France by Besson in France in 1568. He also developed a screw-cutting gauge or plate to be used on lathes. In 1641, the English firm, Hindley of York, improved this device and it became widely used. But still the construction of the screw thread depended upon the eye and skill of the craftsman. Advances occurred in the eighteenth century when Antoine Thiout, around 1750, equipped a lathe with a screw drive allowing the tool carriage to be moved longitudinally semi-automatically. The screws it produced were intended to be used in horological work, the threads being cut by a diamond in hardened steel.

To make fine pitched screws, needed for a wide variety of instruments - such as micrometers a precision lathe of all metal construction was essential. Jesse Ramsden, a maker of mathematical and astronomical instruments, made the first satisfactory screw-cutting lathe in 1770.

In England in 1760, Job and William Wyatt patented a machine that could produce screws automatically but presumably there was little interest as it took 16 years to raise the capital to open a factory. Their machines were simple enough to be operated by children and as one historian wrote, "the Wyatt brothers not only pioneered the use of multipurpose machines to achieve mass production, they were the first to put into place the guiding principal of industrialisation. Their factory was the earliest example of an industrial process designed specifically to shift control over the quality of what was being produced from the skilled artisan to the machine itself."[124] The Wyatts' machine made a screw of higher quality every six or seven seconds compared to several minutes for a handmade screw. Their business was not profitable[125] but their successors were and produced 16,000 screws a day with a team of 30 people. These lathes could not produce the tapered threads we now know and so required pre-drilling before installation.

---

[123] Witold. *One ...*, 72.
[124] Witold. *One ...*, 87.
[125] They were possibly ahead of demand as it took 15 years to raise the capital to build the plant.

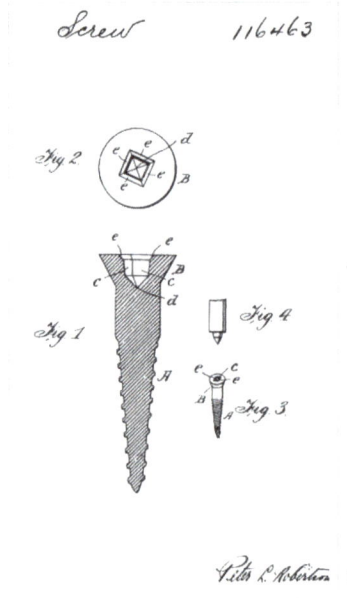

Fig. 41. The first successful alternative to the slotted screw.

Machinery to produce a pointed (but unthreaded) screw was developed in 1849 in Providence, Rhode Island, the centre of the American screw industry which was followed quickly by improved methods. Cullen Whipple (New England Screw Company) and Charles Rogers (American Screw Company) patented different methods of tapering the thread on to the plain shank.[126] The American Screw Company, the largest in America in 1887 could produce each day "about forty thousand gross of wood screws, several tons of rivets, large quantities of machine screws."[127] The screw price was slashed and their use became mainstream. The drawback of the slotted screw which was easily damaged was also started to be addressed through a series of drive types. The first successful alternative was the square drive invented by the Canadian, Peter Robinson in 1907.[128] The new drive was a success and used extensively in the Canadian automotive industry which, like the rest of the world, had wooden frames and product was no longer damaged as, for example, when a screwdriver disengaged with a slotted screw.[129] He resolutely held on to the sole manufacture of the screw limiting its uptake and for many years became a Canadian specialty though now it is very common for domestic decking screws.

In 1933, an American, John Thompson, developed and patented a cross drive screw but could not interest anyone in manufacturing it. It was turned down as not being commercially viable because the punching process would destroy the head.[130] An associate, Henry Philips purchased the design from Thompson, improved it and patented what we know as the Philips head in 1936. He realised from the outset its potential for being power driven but instead of manufacturing it, like Robinson, again tried to license it. Against strong opposition, the CEO of the American Screw Co took up the licence[131] and they were first used in the 1937 Cadillac and within two years all but one American car manufacturer had switched to them.[132] As for the improved head revolutionising the joining of timber, one boat manufacturer estimated "that our operators save between 30 and 60 percent of their time by

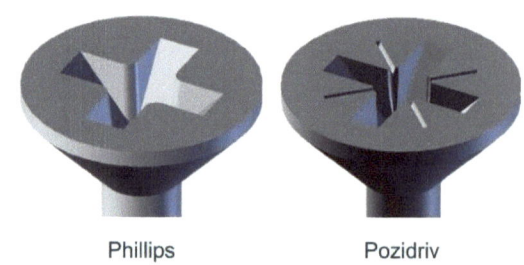

Fig. 42. Philips and Pozidriv compared

---

[126] Witold. *One ...*, 77-8.
[127] Rhode Island Art in Ruins. HTTP: http://www.artinruins.com/arch/?id=historical&pr=americanscrew Date accessed: 4 December 2016. The site is quoting from *History of the State of Rhode Island with Illustrations, 1878* (Philadelphia. Hoag, Wade & Company. 1878). Page number not supplied.
[128] Witold. *One ...*, 80. A square drive was known but it like other alternatives were unsuccessful as they deformed the head. Robinsons method of cold forming made the difference.
[129] Witold. *One ...*, 82.
[130] Witold. *One ...*, 84.
[131] A new President of American Screw named Eugene Clark was captivated by the design despite his engineers' reservations. After Phillips modified the socket's depth so that the punch would be less violent "and some creative motivation from Clark (according to printed reports of the time, he said, "I finally told my head men that I would put on pension all who insisted it could not be done"), the Phillips screw [and all subsequent screws used in modern timber joints] had been born. Lukas Paul. A Twist of Faith An engineer turns an "impossible" idea into manufacturing gold in *CNN Money* Dec 1, 2002. URL: http://money.cnn.com/magazines/fsb/fsb_archive/2002/12/01/333852/index.htm Date accessed: 4 December 2016.
[132] Witold. *One ...*, 84.

using Philips screws."[133] By the use of licensing they were able to capture 75% of the US market by 1944 but licensing brought with it the need to abide by price scheduling. One writer indicates that this made the Philips screw twice the price it should have been.[134] The patent expired in 1966 but The Philips Screw Co and the American Screw Company had been working on a replacement which is termed the Pozidriv. Its design allowed greater torque to be applied without stripping out. Builders frequently confuse the two types and, as a consequence of using the wrong drivers, this can cause damage to the screws. Pozidriv is identified by the small cross at 45 degrees to the main slots. There has been a continual search for improved head types as the conical sides of the Philips and Pozidriv deflect torque upwards which can cause strip out and require more power when driving the screw. Philips are still innovating and licensing new head types and presently have 12 different drives listed on their website.[135]

Fig. 43. Modern screw manufacturing plant in the USA.

---

[133] Witold. *One ...*, 84.
[134] Lampe, Ryan, Petra Moser. Patent Pools: Licencing strategies in the absence of regulation in *History and Strategy*, Edited by Steven Kahl, Michael Cusumano, Brian S. Silverman. (Bingley: Emerald Group, 2012) ,79.
[135] Philips Screw Company. HTTP: http://www.phillips-screw.com/about_us.php. date accessed: 4 December 2016

Joining Timber with Bolts

The invention of the steam engine was as revolutionary for threaded fasteners as it proved for nails. The steam engine became commercially possible when, in 1775, John Wilkinson of Bershaw was able to bore Watt's cylinders with something approaching modern accuracy.[136] The production of steam engines required accurate and interchangeable bolts and nuts. Cylinder boring and accurate bolts only became possible with the introduction of "modern" lathes as, up to then, production of these items had been a very hit and miss affair. The use of dies was well known but they were crude as was the product they produced.[137] Henry Maudsley, (born 1771) an untrained craftsman who possessed "an intuitive power of mechanical analysis and a sense of proportion possessed by few men"[138] would revolutionise not just the production of threaded fasteners but the whole of precision manufacturing.[139] He built and partly designed in 1795 the first lathe with a lead screw operated by changeable gears and the slide rest, one of the greatest inventions of history.[140] Aspects of his lathe existed before but never brought together.[141] In 1800 he built the first screw cutting lathe.

Fig. 44. Maudsley's Screw Cutting Lathe c.1797.

So significant was his work that one writer said "that during the period 1800 to 1810, Mr. Maudsley effected nearly the entire change from the old, imperfect, accidental practice of screw making to the modern, exact, systematic mode now generally followed by engineers: and he pursued the subject of the screw".[142] The ability to produce precision screws meant it was possible to build precision instruments such as surveying tools making roads, railways and waterways possible. Maudsley trained a number of significant engineers including Joseph Whitworth who, in the 1840's, would bring the first attempt to standardise thread shape and pitch, but went a lot further including "standards of measurement and of accuracy and finish were by that time thoroughly recognised and established throughout the country".[143] Finally, a nut made in one country would fit a bolt made in another. While bolts and nuts of uniform size and consistency were available that were fit for purpose, screws still needed significant innovation as was mentioned in the section on screws above.

---

[136] Roe, Joseph. *English and American Tool Builders.* (New York: McGraw-Hill, 1920), 11.
[137] Roe. *English ...*, 38.
[138] Roe. *English ...*, 33
[139] Attributed to Maudsley is the steam engine utilising a crank shaft, a punching machine for punching boiler plates and iron work, flat surfaces and working to an accuracy of 1/1000 of an inch. Roe. *English ...*, 45-7.
[140] Roe. *English ...*, 40.
[141] Woodbury, Robert. *Studies in the History of Machine Tools – History of the Lathe to 1850.* (Cambridge The M.I.T. Press 1972), 99.
[142] Roe. *English ...*, 42.
[143] From the obituary of Sir Joseph Whitworth in *The Times*, January 24, 1887.

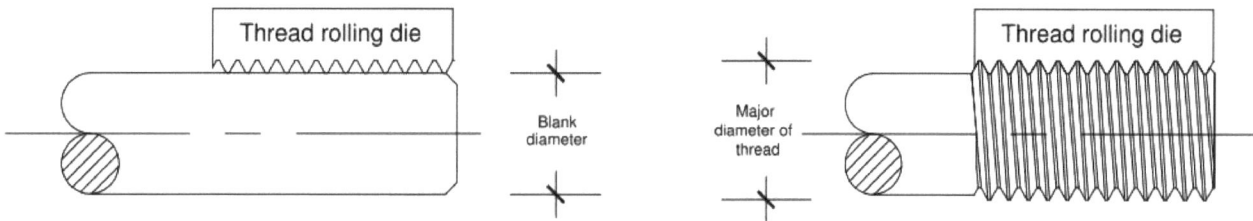

Fig. 45. Rolled threads.

The history of the threaded fastener as described above deals with machining which became exact and provided great flexibility but was time consuming and expensive. It was also wasteful as material had to be removed. Manufacturing of threaded fasteners for timber now involves a threading process where the thread is impressed into a smaller diameter blank and so increasing its diameter. Production of up to 2000 threaded fasteners per minute can be achieved!

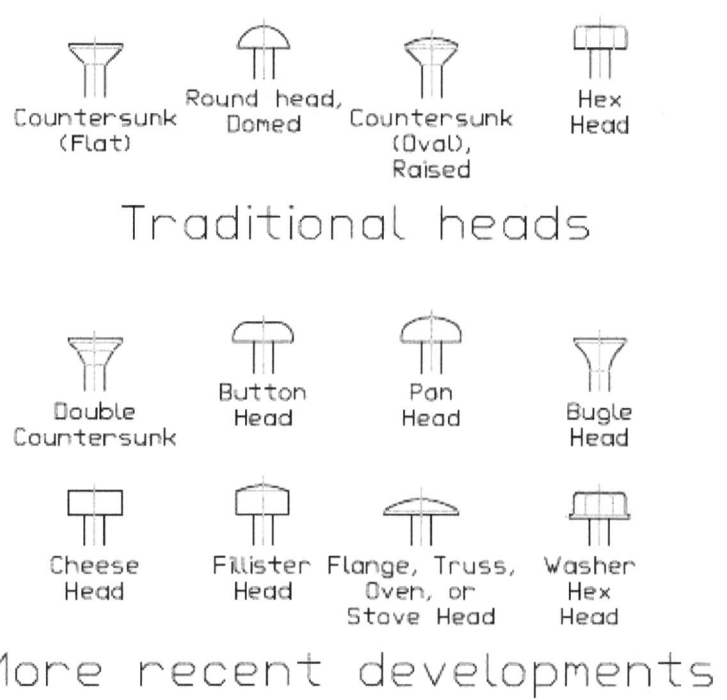

Fig. 46. Screw head types.

Bolts for timber jointing have been limited to the long standing cup head and hex head but screws have far more options. A myriad of head styles and drive types is now available. The points also have become very sophisticated but the majority of wood screws are based around the Type 17 point and the needle point.

The very way that a screw works has now been questioned. Traditionally, a clearance hole was drilled in the piece that the head bore against and an undersize hole was drilled in the other. Should the head snap off, the two pieces part company. Screws are now being made up to an incredible 1500 mm long that are fully threaded and installed without predrilling. The head is just there as a means of providing the drive. There is more on this type of fastener in the chapter Joints in Glued Beams and Panels.

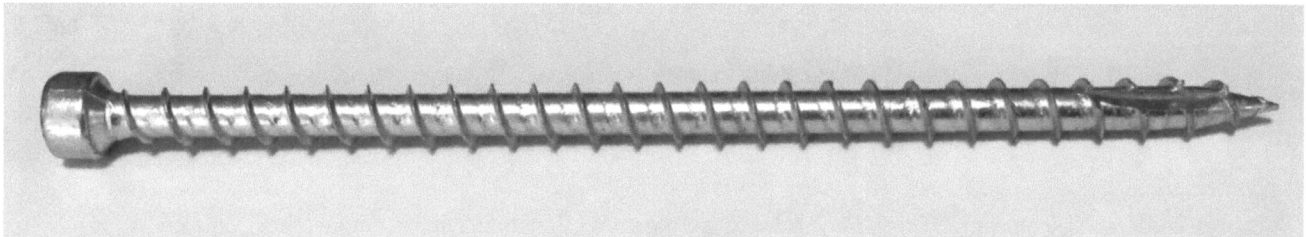

Fig. 47. Fully threaded screw.

An end user can now even consider having screws made to suit their own requirements. When producing decking the author had custom screws made which were 14# 304 grade stainless steel, 85 mm long with a smaller bugle head (batten screws are usually self embedding heads) and wax dipped for easier driving in hardwood. The order quantity was 100,000 units.

There is no reason any longer to accept the status quo in regard to threaded fasteners. A special ongoing need can often be accommodated with a special fastener. The author was frustrated with 10 mm gal coachscrews snapping in hardwood and also being able to be easily vandalised so he patented his own shank profile and added to that a Torx head and utilised high tensile steel. It was roughly equivalent to an M12 bolt and could be driven through a piece of very old ironbark without breaking. Most vandalism is opportunistic so while there may be ready access to a shifting spanner few will have Torx spanners at hand. The thread profile proved very successful in railway ties as well.

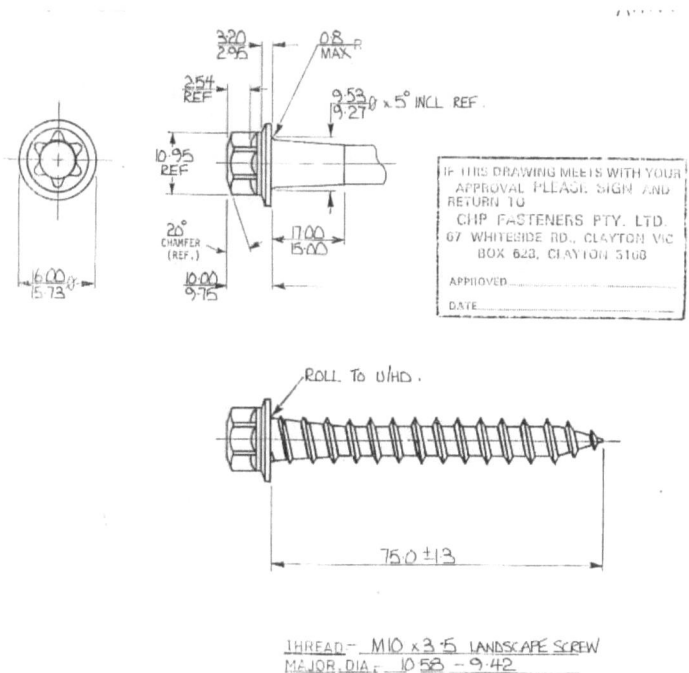

Fig. 48. Thread pattern patented by the author.

Some practicalities in using threaded fasteners

Bolts suffer the same disadvantage as nails as the surface area is relatively small which causes all stresses to concentrate on the small area against which bolts bear. Because of the centralisation of the loads, bolted joints were never as strong as the timber they join so it "always been the custom in design for bolted joints to use members much larger than actually necessary."[144] Larger bolts or more of them help but working against this can be the timber size or the cost of the fasteners. This would change with the introduction of shear plates and split rings which is discussed in the next chapter. Significant increases in load carrying ability can be achieved also by the use of nailplates over the bolt hole.[145]

---

[144] Timber Engineering Company. *Teco Timber Joint Connectors*. (Washington: Timber Engineering Company, 1936), Pages not numbered.
[145] Rogers, C, R Thomson, G. Smith. Nailplate Reinforcement of Bolted Joints in *Pacific Timber Engineering Conference 1994*, 349-352.

Fig. 49. Edge distances are not maintained.

Fig. 50. Possible consequence of edge clearance not being maintained.

With all threaded fasteners whether they be bolts or screws, it is important to maintain end and edge clearances. The picture on the left shows a newly installed 150x100 mm crossarm mounted on its edge on a pole, i.e. the 150 mm face is up. A 20 mm bolt passes through the 100 mm edge. This is common practice with crossarms. The edge clearance required for a perpendicular load under AS1720.1 is four bolt diameters (refer Table Five) but there is allowance in the standard to reduce this if the load is reduced. Even with a reduction in load it would not be wise to reduce below 3 bolt diameters due to possibility of localised defect in the timber such as sloping grain or knots The minimum clearance then is 3x20 mm = 60 mm. The face therefore should be 60 mm + 60 mm = 120 mm. not 100 mm. When the load is in compression and tension the clearance only needs to be 2 bolt diameters i.e. an 80 mm face is needed so a 100 mm face would be acceptable. The picture on the right shows what can occur when three bolt diameter edge clearance is not maintained in a perpendicular load. Any degrade in the bolt hole, a real risk when timber is fully weather exposed, goes from an inconvenience to being critical.

Likewise end clearances are very critical. In tension, the bolt should be 8 diameters from the end though our practice was to add an extra 50 mm to allow for weathering should it be used externally. Sometimes, it takes a lot of thought to be able to achieve the necessary end clearance. Spacings for screws is much simpler than bolts as it does not matter what the timber thickness is or whether it is seasoned or not, the distance remains the same

Spacing Location	Code Requirement D = Screw Diameter	e.g. 6.3 mm dia. Screw (14 gauge)
End Distance	10D	10 x 6.3 = 63 mm
Edge Distance	5D	5 x 6.3 = 32 mm
Between screws along grain	10D	10 x 6.3 = 63 mm
Between screws across grain	3D	3 x 6.3 = 19 mm

Table 5. Minimum screw spacings.[146]

---

[146] Standards Australia. *AS1720.1 – 2010 ...*, Section 4.5.4 and Table 4.4.

Load		Unseasoned	Example 12mm bolt	Seasoned	Example 12mm bolt
Loads parallel to grain					
Edge distance		2D	2 x 12 = 24 mm	2D	2 x 12 = 24 mm
End Distance in tension		8D	8 x 12 = 96 mm	7D	7 x 12 = 84 mm
End Distance in compression		5D	5 x 12 = 60 mm	5D	5 x 12 = 60 mm
End Distance with bending movement		5D	5 x 12 = 60 mm	5D	5 x 12 = 60 mm
Distance between bolts along grain		5D	5 x 12 = 60 mm	5D	5 x 12 = 60 mm
Distance between bolts across grain		4D	4 x 12 = 48 mm	4D	4 x 12 = 48 mm
Loads perpendicular to grain – worked example for 12mm bolt[147]					
Edge distance				4D	4 x 12 = 48 mm
End distance				5D	5 x 12 = 60 mm
Distance between bolts along grain	25 mm thick	b/D ratio 2.08		2.6 D	2.6 x 12 = 31mm
	38 mm thick	b/D ratio 3.95		3.22D	3.2 x 12 – 38 mm
	50 mm thick	b/D ratio 4.16		3.85D	4 x 12 = 48 mm
	75 mm thick	b/D ratio 6.25		5D	5 x 12 = 60 mm
	100 mm thick	b/D ratio 8.33		5D	5 x 12 = 60 mm
Distance between bolts across grain				5D	5 x 12 = 60 mm
Loads acting at an angle of 0-30° to the grain				As for loads parallel to grain	
Loads acting at an angle of 30° to 90° to the grain				As for loads perpendicular to grain	

Table 6. Bolt spacings.[148]

Advantage of screws over bolts in some applications

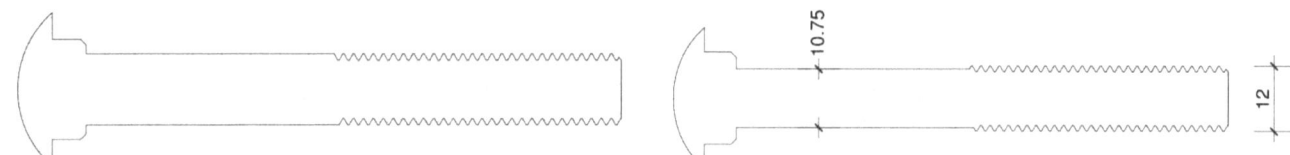

Fig. 51. Perceived bolt shank.   **Fig. 52.** Actual bolt shank.

---

[147] For other sizes divide *b* with is the thickness of the member by D which is the bolt diameter (*b*/D). For a ratio of 2, the distance between the bolts along the grain is 2.5 times the diameter. The distance is pro rata until a ratio of 6 or more is achieved and then the distance is 5D. That is an increase in .625D for each ratio increase. For an M20 bolt fixing a 100 mm thick member the *b*/D ratio is 5. The distance is the base of 2.5D plus 3 times .635D = 4.37D which equals 87.5 mm say 90 mm.

[148] Derived from Standards Australia *AS 1720.1 – 2010* ...., Sections, 4.4.4.2 ,4.4.4.3 and 4.4.4.4.

When installing, for example, a 12 mm bolt into timber, it is necessary to drill oversize and that is generally 2 mm. The hole is not supposed to be more than 10% oversize but 1 mm generally is insufficient clearance and a 13.2 mm drill is not available. As the thread is invariably a rolled thread there isn't a 12 mm shank at the end, it is under 11 mm. This means that there is over 3 mm clearance in one member. For most applications this does not matter but in some it does, such as areas experiencing cyclonic action.

Fig. 53. Screwed instead of bolted.

A screw has a distinct advantage over a bolt in that it is an interference fit and therefore no movement in the joint under extreme situations. It also means that end clearances can be less. Our own preference in building shelters was to screw rather than bolt.

The importance of washers

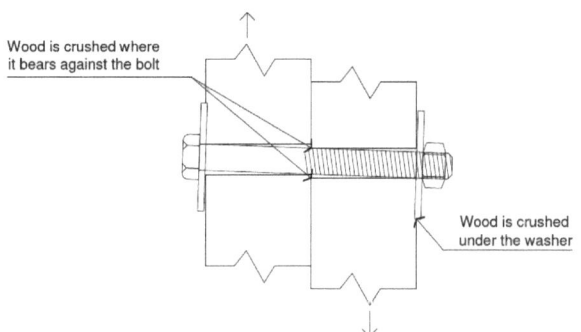

Fig. 54. Action of a bolt under load.

While the shank of a hexagonal headed bolt and a cup head bolt are the same, the load that can be applied to a cup head without washers at both ends is only half that of a hexagonal bolt.[149] The load data in AS1720.1 is for bolts with washers, and as it is impractical to have two different washers as would be needed with cup heads. Hexagonal bolts are used in situations that have a high load.

When loaded in shear a bolted connection's strength comes from the steel shaft bearing against the wood fibres; the larger the bolt, the greater the load that can be carried. But it is more complicated than just that because when the bolt is under load the bolt skews and reduces the surface contact in the critical areas reducing the capacity to carry a load. Skewing, which involves a similar movement of the head can be reduced by the use of washers and the bigger and thicker the washer the less movement there is. Table Six gives the Australian Standard washer sizes.

---

[149] National Association of Forest Industries. *Timber Joint Design -3 Bolts, Coachscrews and Timber Connectors.* (NAFI, 1989), 4. The June 2001 version is available at http://www.timber.net.au/images/downloads/joinery/joint_design3.pdf

Bolt Size	Washer Size (mm)		
	Thickness	Min diameter (Round washer)	Min side length (Square washer)
M6	1.6	30	25
M8	2.0	36	32
M10	2.5	45	40
M12	3.0	55	50
M16	4.0	65	57
M20	5.0	75	65

Table 6. Washer sizes.[150]

Another washer that has proven very effective with unseasoned hardwood is the volute washer, a spiral of stainless steel that collapses within itself when tightened. Shrinkage in unseasoned timber means that bolts are supposed to be retightened but in practice this seldom happens due to cost or impracticality. The volute washer has been used successfully in the overhead power distribution industry for many years and is ideal for items such as handrail posts.

Fig. 55. Volute washer.

The need to consider safety, not just effectiveness

Fig. 56. Protruding bolts are dangerous.

Fig. 57. Safe bolts in public

Fasteners not only have to be effective, but they also have to be safe and not easily vandalised. When starting off selling public landscaping I learnt of a court case where a child received serious injuries from a bolt protruding from a barbecue table used in a public park. The personal cost was high as was the resultant litigation, so all my landscaping was designed so there were no protruding fasteners. This was avoided by use of either tube nuts (Figure 56) or by screws as in Figure 53.

---

[150] Standards Australia. *AS1720.1 – 2010. …*, Table 4.11. The size of washers for larger bolts is not given, only the effective contact area after bending.

Corrosion resistance of self drilling screws

When the Tek patent expired, the Australian market was flooded with low cost, low quality lookalikes. The protective coating could be down to 2-3 microns of electroplated zinc giving only 25% of the corrosion protection of the original ITW Buildex product The implications for corrosion in any timber, let alone treated timber, through inadvertently using poor quality coatings, is obvious. The demand of roofing manufacturers in 1981 that their screws be able to withstand 1000 hours of the standard salt spray test led eventually to AS 3566 – Self Drilling Screws. This Standard was unusual as it is a performance based specification and not a materials specification. Regrettably, this very good standard was withdrawn in 2015. It is understood that large purchasers of screws are still requiring compliance with the old standard and all specifiers would be wise to insist on it. But in practical terms, unless human nature has changed, what brand of screw is used will depend on how much you trust the manufacturer's guarantee.

5. SPLIT RING CONNECTORS AND SHEAR PLATES

Split Rings

The systematic use of timber connectors in the United States came through the intervention of their government which, through the National Committee on Wood Utilization, investigated the use of timber connectors in Europe. Many connectors had emerged in the interwar period on the continent, driven by the need to better utilise their higher cost and more limited availability of timber. Two connectors, with the same general results, were considered to have economic advantages in the United States - split ring and tooth ringed[151] connectors. This was followed up with rigorous testing at the United States Forest Products Laboratory confirming their ability to bring greater utility savings and advantages to the United States resource.[152] These connectors would be used for making what the manufacturer called "primary timber joints" whereas pressed metal connectors, covered further in the book, which followed chronologically, would be used for what called "secondary connections".[153]

At about the same time, to promote the use of timber in the United States, the National Lumber Manufacturing Association (later becoming the National Forest Products Association and still later still the American Forest & Paper Association) decided in 1933 that it was necessary to determine the physical properties of their timber. This involved establishing a laboratory, the Timber Engineering Company (TECO)[154], to undertake physical testing. The association of what was initially a testing organisation with timber connectors started in 1934 when it purchased the rights to a split ring connector from a German manufacturer.

It is difficult to appreciate the significance of these connectors in an age where we have so much choice. Getting a successful connection between large section timber and gluelams had been a problem. However, with the widespread availability of such connectors, designers finally had well researched and known strength values for joints and for the timber they connected. The new connections could be two or even three times stronger than ordinary bolt and plate connections. In fact, for the first time, it was possible to have a joint that was as strong as the timber itself. The end result was claimed to be a 20% reduction in the volume of timber required and a lowering of the timber grade. The cost benefits continued with quicker construction times and a lowering of the skill needed.[155]

The Council of Scientific and Industrial Research (predecessor of the CSIRO) was established in the 1930's and timber engineering was a major research area between 1935 and 1938. They "introduced shear connector joint technology and modern glue lamination techniques. Both were extensively used overseas but remained little used in Australia."[156] Despite their best efforts timber technology up to 1941 was mainly traditional "English practice, with mortise and tenon joints in king and queen post

---

[151] No longer available in its original form.
[152] Timber Engineering Company. *Teco ,,,.* Pages not numbered.
[153] Timber Engineering Company. *Timber for Recreational Buildings*. (Washington: Timber Engineering Company, 1950), 21 available at https://ia802700.us.archive.org/18/items/TimberForRecreationalBuildings_2/TimberEngineering-CoCca35692.pdf
[154] TECO is a name that was long associated with timber connectors in Australia.
[155] Timber Engineering Company. *Teco ,,,.* Pages not numbered.
[156] Nolan. *Extraordinary ...,*

trusses."[157]

The coming of the Second World War, and with it the need for larger yet simpler structures alongside the imperative of using materials very efficiently, would force the introduction of timber engineering and improved connectors into the Australian market led, of course, by the recent United States developments.

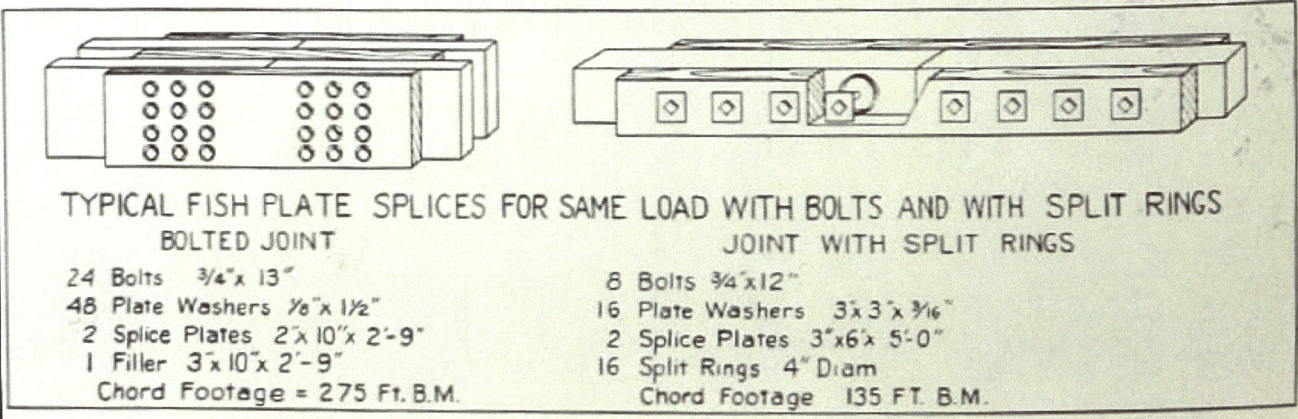

Fig. 58. The claimed difference between a bolted joint and one with split ring connectors.[158]

Instead of the joint solely relying on a bolt or lag screw for restraint, a split ring allows higher loads to be applied and be transferred over a larger area and, in doing so, improve the joint's efficiency. This is the same effect as a large diameter bolt but without the need to remove a large volume of timber. Split rings are particularly useful if there are edge and end clearance restrictions. The correct size bolt and washer which clamps the joint together, though not involved in the transfer of shear, is critical for a successful connection.

Fig. 59. Split ring in operation

Fig. 60. Split ring groove tool.

---

[157] Nolan. *Extraordinary ...*,
[158] Timber Engineering Company. *Teco ,,,.* Pages not numbered.

This connector, which greatly increased the effectiveness of a bolted joint, was initially a square sided ring dowel[159] which required considerable clearance in the groove to assemble. This clearance could result "in the creation of what is termed an inelastic slip[160] in the joint which leads to deformation of the ultimate timber structure under load".[161] In an attempt to improve the connector by dealing with the gap, a new design with a small concave central portion in the form of a shallow V pointing outwards was introduced.[162] This is the ring that was used in the construction of the largest timber structures ever built, the blimp[163] hangars used by the US Navy in World War 2. Unfortunately, the clearances were still too large and "In some of these, the inelastic slip in the timber joints … contributed to sags in the trusses used in aircraft hangars to such an extent that they have caused the hangar doors to bind, making the structure unusable".[164]

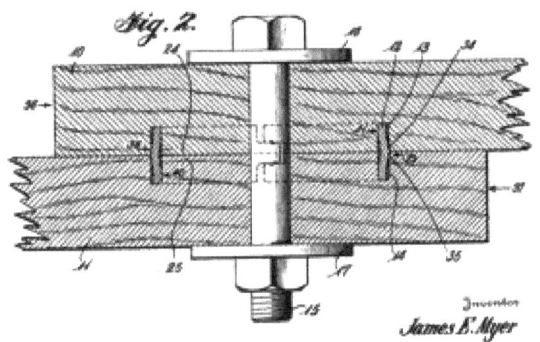
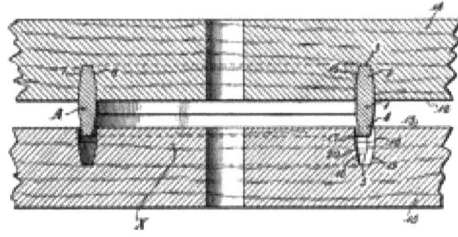

Fig. 61. Improved ring connector 1939.   **Fig. 62** Final ring connector 1945.

The final version of the split ring connector solved the clearance problem by introducing a taper to the top and bottom of the ring which fitted into a matching tapered groove. This achieved a no clearance joint at the same time as having an easy assembly (and reassembly if needed) joint. Inelastic slip was reduced by as much as 50% over the earlier designs.[165]

As has been mentioned, split ring connectors made possible the construction of the world's largest timber structures as far as volume is concerned, the airship hangars built in the United States during World War 2.

---

[159] US Patent 1409320 A, granted March 14, 1922.
[160] Now simply referred to as "slip" in Australia
[161] US Patent US 2377156 A, granted May 29, 1945.
[162] US Patent 2150141 A, granted March 7, 1039.
[163] A blimp is a powered, steerable airship that takes its shape from the pressure of gas within its envelope.
[164] US Patent US 2377156 A, granted May 29, 1945.
[165] US Patent US 2377156 A, granted May 29, 1945.

Fig. 63. Views of Tillamook blimp hangar.

A total of 17 airship hangars were built during the war, each hangar housed 8 airships that were 80 metres long. Because there was a steel shortage during the war, wood was chosen and the resulting hangars were reported also to be the largest clear span timber structures built at that time. After the prototype was built, it only took a year to build the remaining seventeen, testimony to timber's versatility. The clear space inside the hangar at Tillamook (now an air museum) is: span 90 metres, length 320 metres, and height 53 metres. The front doors are supported off 93 metre span timber box beams supported off 71 metre high concrete columns. The sister hanger to this at Tillamook was apparently completed in 27 working days!

How do you achieve such large spans? This is building on a scale several times larger than we saw in the ubiquitous WW2 aircraft hangars that could be seen around Australia. The smaller Australian hangars were generally built from lineal 100x50 and 75x50 mm with 75x25 mm bracing and simply nailed together yet the technology used in them was ground breaking and utilised timber up three times more efficiently than it had been before. The connections for the blimp hangars had to be much better than this.

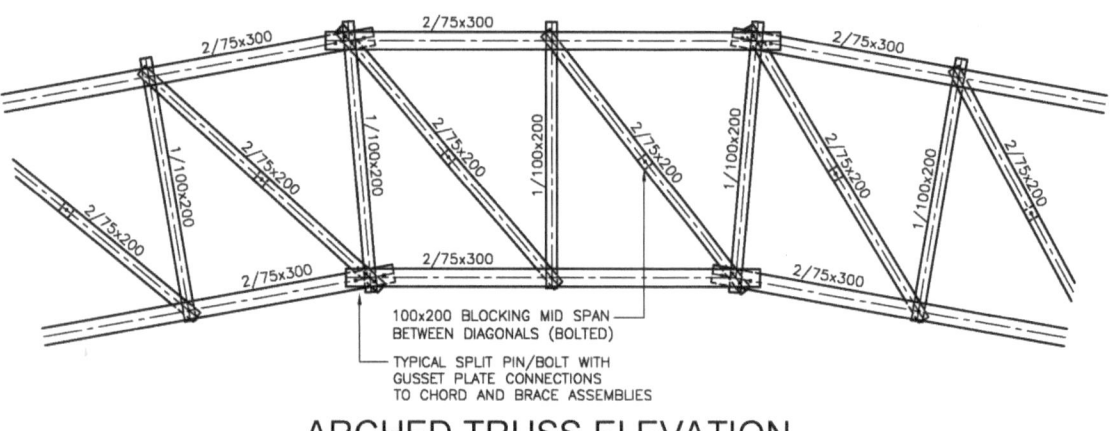

Fig. 64. Detail of Tillamook hangar construction. Redrawn from Navy Department, Bureau Yards and Docks, Lighter-Than-Air Hangar. Drawing 212817.

Structurally, the hangars feature 51 inverted catenary arch[166] truss with a Pratt truss (refer Figure 84) configuration with the truss frames at about 6 metre centres. The cords (double 350x75 mm for the top and double 300x75 mm for the bottom) are sawn Oregon joined by an earlier version split-ring connectors and bolts. There was 24,000 m³ of timber used at Tillamook, all of which was treated with fire-retardant salts (of dubious efficacy). These split rings proved to be very efficient, but not entirely trouble free means of joining timbers which led to our present tapered shape.

---

[166] A catenary is the U-like curve that an idealized hanging chain (the word is derived from the Latin for chain) or cable assumes under its own weight when supported only at its ends. It is superficially similar to a parabola.

Split rings are manufactured in imperial sizes in diameters of 63 mm (2-1/2″) and 100 mm (4″) from hot-rolled carbon steel for use with 13 mm (1/2″) and 19 mm (3/4″) diameter bolts respectively. A single split ring insets into both the pre-cut grooves in the wood surface being joined. A tongue and groove split in the ring permits the ring to deform slightly under load (or change of moisture content) so that all contact areas distribute load, and the special wedge shape on both sides of the ring eases insertion and ensures a tight fitting joint when the ring is fully seated in the grooves.

Fig. 65. Split rings.

Split ring installation requires close supervision. In practice, the joint is assembled and the central bolt hole is drilled. The joint is then dissembled and the hole becomes the guide for the post of the grooving tool. The joint is reassembled with the rings in place. Once assembled the rings are not visible. The inspection would check that the groove is formed correctly and to check that the rings have actually been installed!

Fig. 66. Using split rings on a "normal" building.

None of us are going to build an airship hangar so is there a use of split rings on smaller structures? Figure 66 shows the rafters being attached to the posts in the author's office where they were connected with split rings. The rafters are 250 mm deep which means about 15 mm shrinkage overall in the rafter while there will be no shrinkage in the post. If the designer had used two bolts, the holes really should be elongated and that causes all manner of problems, least of all is how do you actually do it? But a single bolt with a split ring solved the shrinkage problem and gave a joint without any clearance. Note how I have used galvanised split rings. Most US split rings are sold without corrosion protection and galvanising is only recommended if the timber is treated or in a moist environment. Because of the acidity of Australian hardwoods I would advise that they always be galvanised for our conditions. Stainless is preferable but are not available. The split rings at Tillamook are only black steel and are corroding but, to be fair, it was only meant to be a temporary structure and never intended to end up on a register of heritage listed buildings.

The use of split rings in bridges is not recommended unless they can be effectively protected from the weather as in a covered bridge. In my early days of bridge building I did have plans for a truss using, if I recall correctly, mainly 150x50 mm and with everything connected with split rings. But before we could build our first bridge to this design our consultant rang us to tell us that the certification was no longer valid. He advised that, after a failure, the design value of the split rings was reduced to a third for external work.[167] This highlights the problem with any timber structure of how to develop a strong connection with small timber sizes that will withstand the elements for over 50 years.

I cannot see that these connectors are available in Australia any longer but they are readily available from the US. One such company is Portland Bolt.[168] Probably what worked against this and the other connectors developed at this time was simply that Australia did not and still does not have a culture of turning to timber for large structures.

Shear Plates

Fig. 67. Beam sagging despite large steel size used to replace broken nailplates.

Some careless employees kept diving the masts of the forklifts into the roof beam of one of my sawmill buildings. This, in turn, dislodged the light nailplates that had up to then been keeping everything together and importantly, straight. After propping the beam straight, I had two lengths of 3.0m long 150x75 unequal angle installed in place of the two light plates. They quickly sagged as clearance in the holes further enlarged as the load came back on them. This dry hardwood would have been an ideal application for shear plates, another way of transferring loads into timber and so reducing the number of bolts required.

---

[167] The exact details are not known but it was recalled this way, "At one time split rings and shear plates were downgraded because of a failure and the distance from the ends of the member were increased especially for tension members. Additionally the strength was downgraded if there was a moisture problem i.e. weather exposure, swimming pools etc." Pierce, James. *Pers. Com.* September 9, 2015.

[168] "These products are still used regularly in the US, we've sold 20,000 split rings and 115,000 shear plates in the last 12 months. I can also say that we've had decent sized inquiries from all over the world, including Australia in the last year." Erde-Wollheim, Nate. *Pers. Com.* April 25, 2016. Nate is responsible for sales of these items with Portland Bolt.

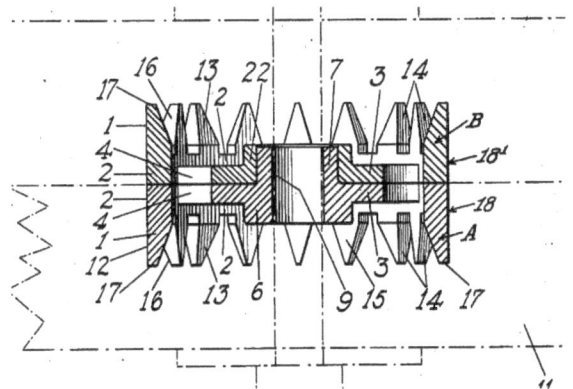

Fig. 68. Original shear plate set – timber to timber.

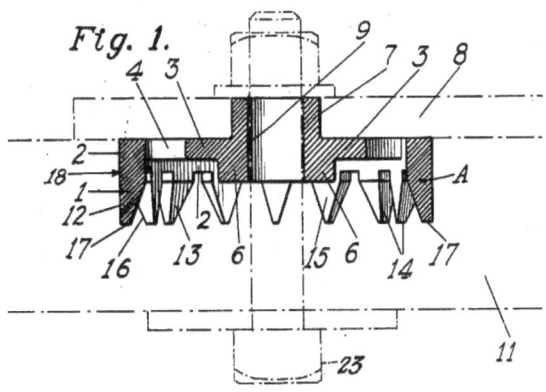

Fig. 69. Original shear plate set – timber to steel

Fig. 70. Shear plates from USA, 2 5/8" and 4 "

Shear plates were developed by TECO in the 1930's along with other timber connectors including spike grids. Unlike split rings which are only a timber to timber connection, shear plate can be used in steel to timber applications. Because of this they found application in structures that were prefabricated and joined with plates.

Like split rings, shear plates have also undergone a process of change since first patented as illustrated in Figures 68 and 69.[169] Then, two versions were considered, one for wood to wood assembly and the other for wood to steel. The teeth may have pressed into American softwoods but would have barely touched an Australian hardwood. Fortunately, the teeth were soon discarded as was the smaller centre boss that fitted into the timber, at least on the smaller plates. The one plate is now used for both timber to timber and timber to steel applications.

---

[169] US Patent 2092684 A. Granted September 7, 1937.

Shear Plates are manufactured in two Imperial sizes: 2-5/8″ (67 mm) diameter in pressed steel for use with 3/4″ (19 mm) bolts or lag screws, and 4″ (100 mm) diameter in malleable iron for use with 3/4″ or 7/8" (19 mm or 22 mm) bolts or lag screws. While the connection is much better than just a simple bolted connection, unlike a split ring, a zero clearance joint is not achieved so there can be movement in the joint and slip was reported in Australian structures, particularly ones using unseasoned hardwood. Despite Oregon pine shrinking up to 5% and the 100 plate not shrinking at all, they work satisfactorily in this timber when unseasoned. You would expect that the same thing will happen in spotted gum at 6% shrinkage but perhaps needing extra end and side clearance. When the shrinkage is 12% something has to give and it will not be the plate.

Fig. 71. Shear plates used on timber to timber joint.

Fig. 72. A 39.6m hardwood truss using shearplates under construction at Tocumwal, NSW during World War 2.

Fig. 73. Truss made with Shear plate connectors at Werribee aerodrome.

An example of the use of shear plate construction is the heritage listed Werribee aerodrome hangars constructed during World War Two. These are an American design, re-engineered from pine to Australian hardwood with clear spans reaching 130 ft (39.6 m).[170] Like the Igloo, timber farming was again used as steel was in short supply. One author wrote "Architecturally these structures are unique as they are the first long span trusses recorded that use timber as tension web members. They [were in 1996] the longest clear span gable shaped timber truss buildings known in Australia."[171] Similar trusses were built elsewhere including Tocumwal.

The 96 ft (29.3 m) hangar used a double 8x3 inch (200x75 mm) for the top cord a double 6x3 inch (150x75 mm) for the bottom cord. The main diagonals reduced from double 6x3 inch (150x75 mm) at the centre to 4x3 inch (100x75 mm) and ancillary bracing is single 4x2 inch (100x50 mm). These trusses were, in a sense, experimental as up until then timber in major projects had been seasoned but there was no longer time for this. Unseasoned timber had to be used and the engineers had to learn how to overcome the difficulties that caused.[172]

---

[170] Hankins, Alan, Thanh Ho. *Werribee Satellite Aerodrome Hangars – Nomination for Heritage Recognition.* (Engineering Heritage Victoria, 2005), 9.
[171] Nolan. *Forgotten ...*, 20.
[172] Allied Works Council, *Report of Activities: 26/2142 to 30!6/43.* (Melbourne) 345. Quoted in Nolan. *Forgotten ...*, 13.

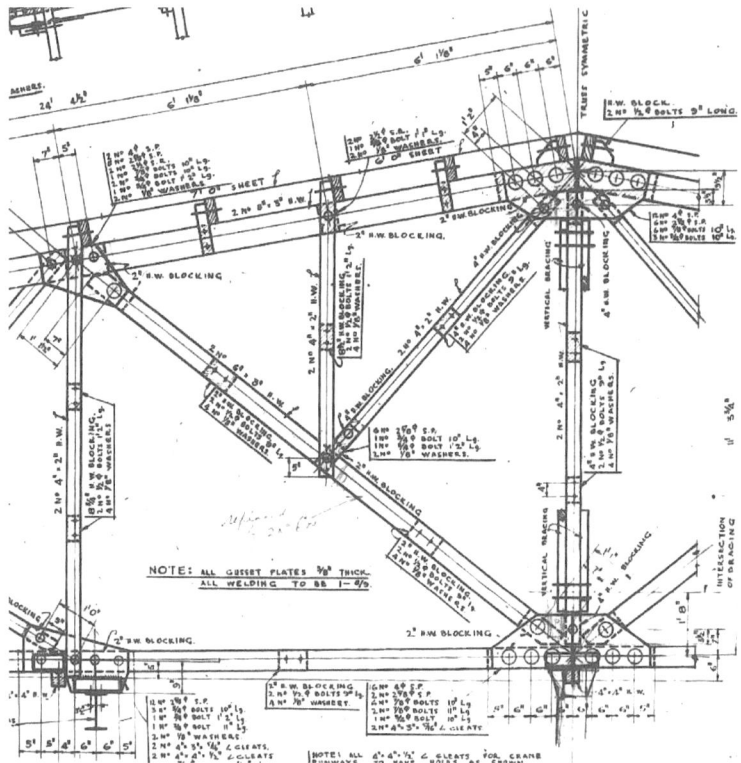

Fig. 74. Detail of truss in 29.3 m Werribee Hangar.

While no problems were reported with the shorter 96 ft spans, the 130 ft truss initially had considerable problems. The 130ft (39. 6 m) span trusses were constructed with a straight-line camber of 8 ins (200 mm) at the centre of the span but when measured 9 months after construction, deflections from the cambered position ranged from 184 mm to 238 mm.[173] Deflection, roughly the quarter points of the span were the lowest, giving a double festooned appearance. This required the trusses to be propped and re-cambered. Gregory Nolan speculated that "It is probable that the stresses allowed were just too great for satisfactory performance with green hardwood."[174] With the seasoning of the timber no further problems were reported and those of both lengths that were inspected in 1992 were performing satisfactorily.[175]

---

[173] Nolan. *Forgotten ...*, 20.
[174] Nolan. *Forgotten ...*, 20.
[175] Nolan. *Forgotten ...*, 20.

Toothed Ring Connectors

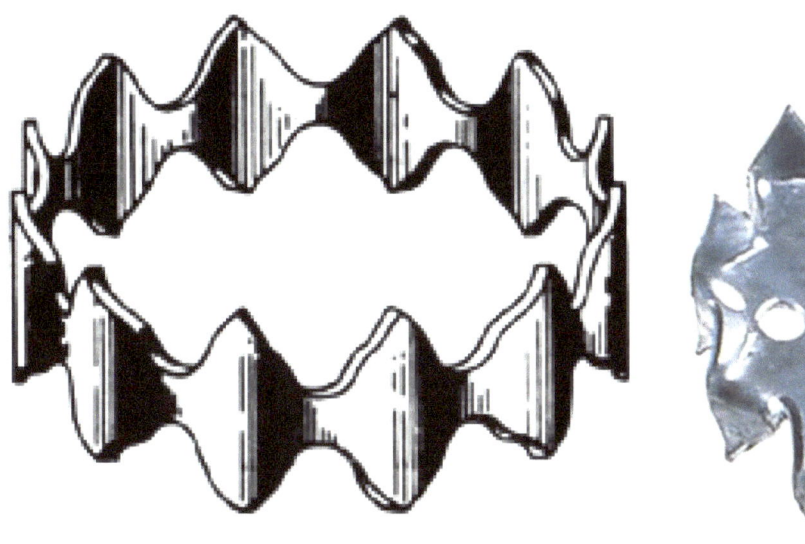

Fig. 75. Original toothed ring connector

Fig. 76. Modern double sided tooth plate connector.

The second connector adopted along with the split ring in an attempt to revolutionise timber joints was the toothed ring connector. It was made from 16 gauge steel (1.59 mm) and worked in the same way as the split ring except that it did not suit prefabrication. After drilling for the bolt, the ring was installed between the pieces to be joined. A high strength bolt was then used to tighten the joint and force the ring into the timber. The bolt was then removed and replaced with a standard bolt.[176] These particular connectors are no longer available but have been replaced with a revised item now termed a tooth plate connector. The new design is available as a two sided version as shown in Figure 76 or as single sided versions to suit prefabrication. These were available in Australia but it appears this is no longer the case. However they can be easily sourced from the United States or the United Kingdom. These connectors will work with pine but not with our hardwoods.

---

[176] Timber Engineering Company. *Teco ,,,.* Pages not numbered.

Case History

Fig. 77. Laminated log bridge with shear keys.

Fig. 78. Shear plates with installation tool.

In my early days of bridge building we produced a 14 metre long bridge using laminated logs. It was extremely heavy but did give us a timber option for spans greater than 10 metres which was the longest we supplied as a simple girder bridge. The girders had one side faced, put together, drilled and then dissembled. Shear plates were fitted and the logs checked to house timber keys. Split rings were considered too light as there were not a large number of bolts, and also considered too difficult to fit. Increasing the bolts was not an option especially as each bolt meant drilling through 500 mm of hardwood. The timber keys were well seasoned and, when reassembled, set in resin so there was no clearance. Minus the resin and shear plates, this was common construction detailing for NSW railway bridges.

Though a lot of effort was made to make a good connection, it was simply impossible to achieve composite action with the two logs and the plate did little more than reinforce the bolt hole and stop it elongating. The clearance in the bolt holes meant the girders eventually had to sag. Realising this from the beginning, I simply accommodated for it by building a 75 mm camber in the deck so it settled relatively straight.

Fig. 79. Forming groove for shear key.

Fig. 80. Installing shear key.

A change of engineers saw a different approach leading to a real composite action being achieved, The shear plates and wooden keys were dispensed with. Instead, the bridge was simply assembled and bolted. A machine was constructed that would put a 15x105 mm groove through the interface of the log. Then a 16x100 mm galvanised plate was driven through the groove. It was a success but, ever the pessimist, I still put the 50-75 mm hog in the deck.

6. NAIL PLATES

Trusses - A Brief History

Trusses have been with us since antiquity, possibly as early as the sixth century B.C. but certainly by the third century B.C. The tie beam truss is just a simple triangle with the rafters in compression and the tie beam in tension making a coherent system. This may well have originated in the Greek shrines in Sicily[177] where the builders used larger unsupported spans than those used on the Greek mainland.[178] While there is little evidence that the Greeks capitalised on the trusses ability to deliver large open spaces, the Romans certainly did utilise them. They were able to span over 30 metres by the time of Augustus.[179] Unfortunately, we no longer have evidence available about how these joints were constructed. One researcher commented "There is no question, however, that the timber truss was extremely strong and for this reason is still a fundamental component of modern timber framing."[180] For all their innovation, there is little or no evidence of any engineering theory being employed and, as floor frames were generally heavier than needed, the same is likely to have applied to the trusses.[181]

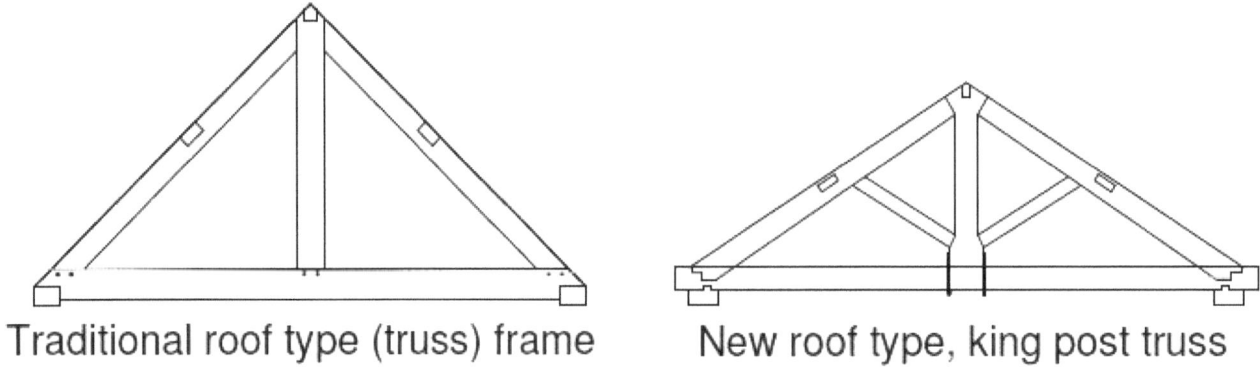

Fig. 81. Transition of king post truss.

In these early trusses, the ceiling beam had to carry the full load of the roof with their own bearing capacity. Some scholars think that the tie beam (bottom cord) in some of these trusses from antiquity could have been as deep as 500 mm![182] While these timbers may well have been available in a world that still had large almost virgin forests, it was not sustainable. We see over the intervening years the timber sizes decreasing and now modern builders who wish to take advantage of a truss's obvious strength must do so with much smaller sizes and improved truss designs and connections. This

---

[177] The three temples in Sicily with the greatest spans are those of Olympian Zeus, Hercules and E which span 12.8, 11.84 and 11.7m respectively. The three largest unsupported spans in classical Greece were the Parthenon, the Erechtheion and the Treasury of Gela at 11.05, 9.8 and 9.68 m respectively.
[178] Ulrich. *Roman...*, 140.
[179] The Odeum in Aosta, Italy, which dates from Augustus's period, spanned 30.49 metres and the throne room of Flavius c. 92 AD spanned 31.67 metres.
[180] Ulrich. *Roman ...*, 140.
[181] Ulrich. *Roman ...*, 139.
[182] Ulrich. *Roman ...*, 139

improvement was started with the development of the king post truss. Initially, in ancient Greece this was a compression member where the post was attached to the ceiling beam and supported the weight of the rafters, being fitted under or into them where they met at the apex. In this arrangement the load on the ceiling beam was increased. But the king post design transitioned whereby the post extended to the top of the apex and the rafters fitted into the post, in effect hanging the post from the rafters which could then be used to support what is now a tie beam.[183] Members that were subject to bending were now primarily axially loaded which transferred much greater loads into the base of the rafter where it joined the ceiling beam. This loading allowed for smaller sizes which are needed for larger spans. To this in time were added different diagonal and post arrangements but the approach to the design of trusses was still empirical.

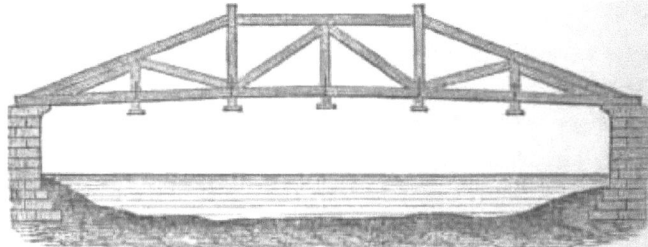

Fig. 82. Palladio's 36 m bridge over the Cismon River.

Fig. 83. Trajan's 33 m bridge over the Danube (from Trajan's column).

The start of the transition from empirical design to a scientific approach is often attributed to Andrea Palladio[184] and his widely disseminated 1570 treatise *i quattro libri dell'Architettura* where he describes a number of timber bridges without intermediate supports. Palladio claims them as "inventions" as he believed them to be different to anything seen previously. His book contains the oldest detailed designs for bridge trusses including that of the Cismon River which spanned 36 metres.[185] The Romans were able to achieve bridge spans of 33 metres but these were not simply supported structures but gained the benefit of continuity from the adjacent truss (refer Figure 83). The joints he designed would not be improved upon for at least 200 years but their very labour intensive nature highlights the difficulty of making effective connections for large span trusses. Another contribution was the development of modularity with standard sized members (for Cismon bridge 360

---

[183] Rinke, M. T, Kotnik. The Changing concept of truss design caused by the influence of Science. Structures and Architecture CSA 2010 - 1st International Conference on Structures & Architecture, July 21-23 July, 2010 in Guimaraes, Portugal Edited by Paulo J. Cruz, S (CRC Press 2010), 1960. Available: http://www.schwartz.arch.ethz.ch/Publikationen/-Dokumente/truss_science_rinke.pdf

[184] He gave his name to Palladian architecture which drew from classical temple architecture and based on symmetry and perspective.

[185] Tampone, Gennaro, Francesca Funis. Palladio's Timber Bridges. *Proceedings of the First International Congress on Construction History, Madrid*, 20th-24th January 2003, ed. S. Huerta, Madrid: I. Juan de Herrera, SEdHC, ETSAM, A. E. Benvenuto, COAM, F. Dragados, 2003. 1912. Being able to incorporate printed images in a book revolutionised the dissemination of ideas.

mm high and 270 mm wide) and components that could be prefabricated and quickly assembled.[186]

Trajan's bridge was essentially an arch built of timber instead of stone and at the beginning of the 19th century "arch structures were considered the most suitable structural system for large span [timber] bridges".[187] In the arch there were, in effect, no joints compared to the multiplicity of joints and greater deflection in the truss. But the rapid expansion of railways in North America brought a new approach. The profit driven and highly competitive environment forced builders to seek solutions that required a minimum amount of time and effort to achieve the desired outcome.[188] Wood and labour were relatively inexpensive and steel was expensive so these solutions were frequently wooden. This would lead to a rush of new truss types, many bearing the names of their inventors. Some of these are:

- Burr arch truss (Thomas Burr, patented 1817)
- Town truss (Ithiel Town, patented 1820)
- Howe truss (William Howe, patented 1840)
- Bowstring arch truss (Squire Whipple, patented 1841)
- Pratt truss (Thomas and Caleb Pratt, invented 1844)
- Warren truss (James Warren, patented 1848).

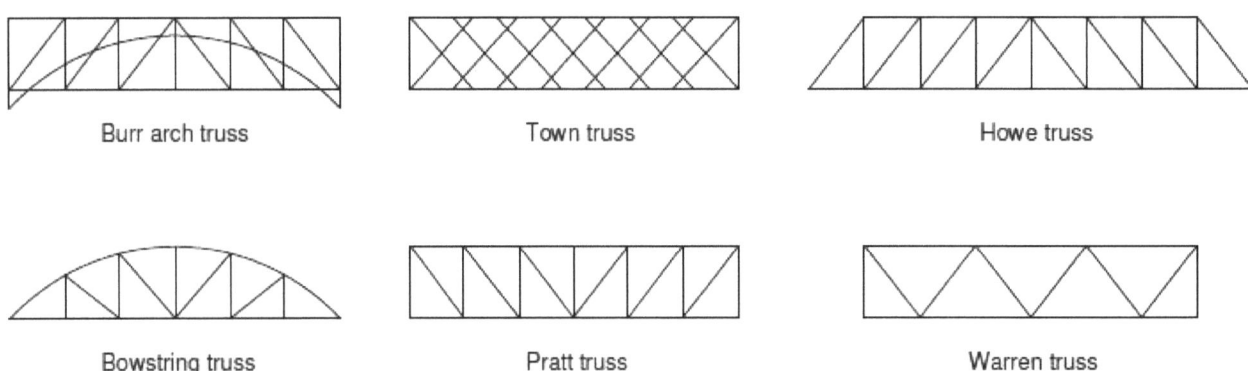

Fig. 84. Illustrations of different truss types.

It should be noted that these trusses predate the first scientific publications on the theory of trusses which were not released until 1851 and were in German.[189]

Trusses in Domestic Construction

So how did the principals behind labour intensive, large and costly monumental and commercial structures with large member sizes and expensive fasteners and connections become the dominant method of construction for very price sensitive domestic roof construction? This is an even more loaded question when it has been maintained that the old technology of pitching a roof as opposed to using roof trusses can still be a better approach. One of Australia's most awarded builders claims that a

---

[186] Tampone. *Palladio's ...*, 1917.
[187] Rinke. *Changing ...*, 1961.
[188] Rinke. *Changing ...*, 1962.
[189] Rinke. *Changing ...*, 1963. Rinke claims that an earlier essay by Whipple, inventor of the bowstring arch truss in 1847 went virtually unnoticed.

conventional pitched roof can be more economical and allow more flexibility with complex roof shapes but it does require exceptionally skilled carpenters (at least by modern standards).[190] The pressed metal connectors which we are about to discuss are the mainstay of Australian construction but often can be replaced with the old but more labour intensive technology of metal straps and bolts. It could also be asked why it took over 100 years from the beginning of the scientific understanding of trusses to the first nailplated trusses to emerge. The technology required was available as hydraulic rams for pressing were available commercially in the 1850's and low cost metal stamping dates from the 1880's.

The improvements in truss design following World War One as seen in the previous chapter in the discussion of split rings and shear plates needed for large trusses had little impact on the much smaller scale domestic housing. It could even be argued that there was initially no single compelling need to change from the hand pitched roof. What would change matters was the Second World War and the construction boom following and particularly the work of two men William Levitt and John Calvin Jureit. Both these men would be likened to Henry Ford in the way they transformed housing from being crafted one at a time into an assembly line construction.[191]

Fig. 85. Levittown PA. The beginning of suburbia and modern housing construction

Housing growth declined in the US during the depression (1929 to the late 1930's) which was then followed by four years of war when again little housing was constructed as the war effort consumed all available resources. After the war, young couples with high birth rates had easy access to much needed low interest loans which drove an almost insatiable demand for low cost housing. William Levitt, a builder, along with his father Abraham and brother Alfred, purchased inexpensive land outside of town limits and from 1947

---

[190] Pingel, Derek. *Pers. Com.* 2 July 2013. Derek was National Award winner for the Australian Quality Home Builder Award 1996-99 and was president of the Queensland Master Builders Association.

[191] Merullo, Roland. J. Calvin Jureit, Inventor Who Transformed Home Building, Dies at 87 Sept. 18, 2005 New York Times. URL: http://www.nytimes.com/2005/09/18/us/j-calvin-jureit-inventor-who-transformed-home-building-dies-at-87.html?_r=0 Date accessed: December 15, 2016 and Raizman. David. *History of Modern Design: Graphics and Products Since the Industrial Revolution.* (London Laurence King Publishing 2003), 305.

built planned communities of up to 17,000 new homes in New York, New Jersey and Pennsylvania. The suburbs were invented. William had learnt mass production strategies building military housing for the navy during the war. The homes in his Levittown communities were built of precut but not preassembled components on concrete slabs instead of foundations with basements by teams that had one of twenty-six specialised task. Levitt's homes could be produced in under six weeks and though inexpensive (initially $7990 which was three times the average annual wage) were well built and incorporated all mod cons including a TV and hi-fi. The down payment could be as little as one dollar and there was little risk to the builder as the mortgages were government guaranteed.[192] Levitt denied he was a builder but claimed instead to be a manufacturer. The efficiency of Levitt's construction methods quickly led to it becoming the industry standard in the US and later Australia. With the transformation of house construction from a cottage industry to a major manufacturing process the scene was set for a revolution in prefabrication using trusses and premade frames.

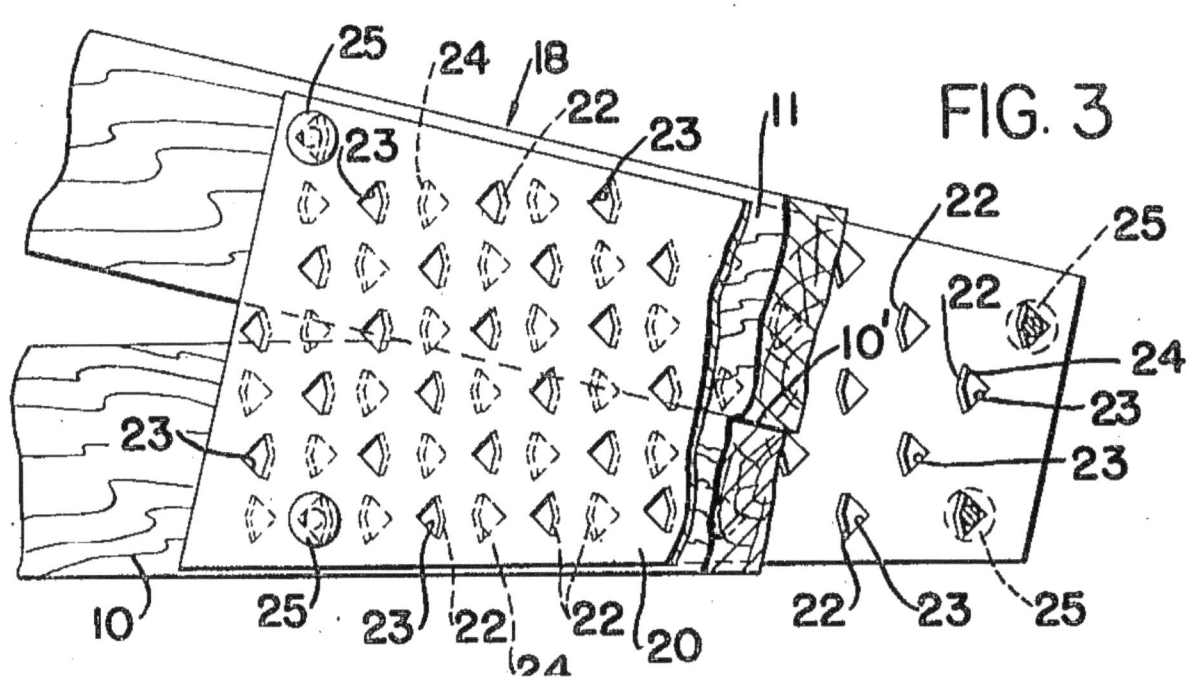

Fig. 86. The first nailplate connector for roof trusses invented by Carol Sanford, US Patent 2827676A filed 1954.

While Levitt did not use trusses, these were available as the need to quickly construct prefabricated military housing with labour having limited skills had dictated their use. Originally the trusses were simply nailed or joined with plywood plates which were glued and nailed to dimensioned timber and later, to speed up prefabrication, predrilled steel plates were used with nails. Both the plate options were labour intensive. In 1952, A. Carol Sandford, a Detroit architect who wanted to reduce the labour in truss construction is credited with developing the first toothed and press installed metal nailplate called

---

[192] Raizman. David. *History ...*, 305 and Marshall, Colin. Levittown, the prototypical American suburb – a history of cities in 50 buildings, day 25 .*The Guardian* (Australian edition) April 28 2015. Note that the deposit was generally $100.

the Gri-P-Late.[193] It is barely recognisable as a nailplate as we presently know them as apart from being triangular, it had short triangular teeth. The way it worked was also very different as Sandford believed it was important not to shear the wood fibres.[194] While this plate was a marked improvement in time and effectiveness, the labour involved was still too high as it still required extra hand driven nails. A key aspect of this invention was the need to utilise readily available and very economic 100x50 mm timber which is a remarkable reduction in material over the 150x50 mm used in the conventionally pitched roofs of Levitt.[195] The original plate had the single triangular tooth as opposed to later plates with a number of teeth protruding from a round hole (refer Figure 89 showing historical plates).[196]

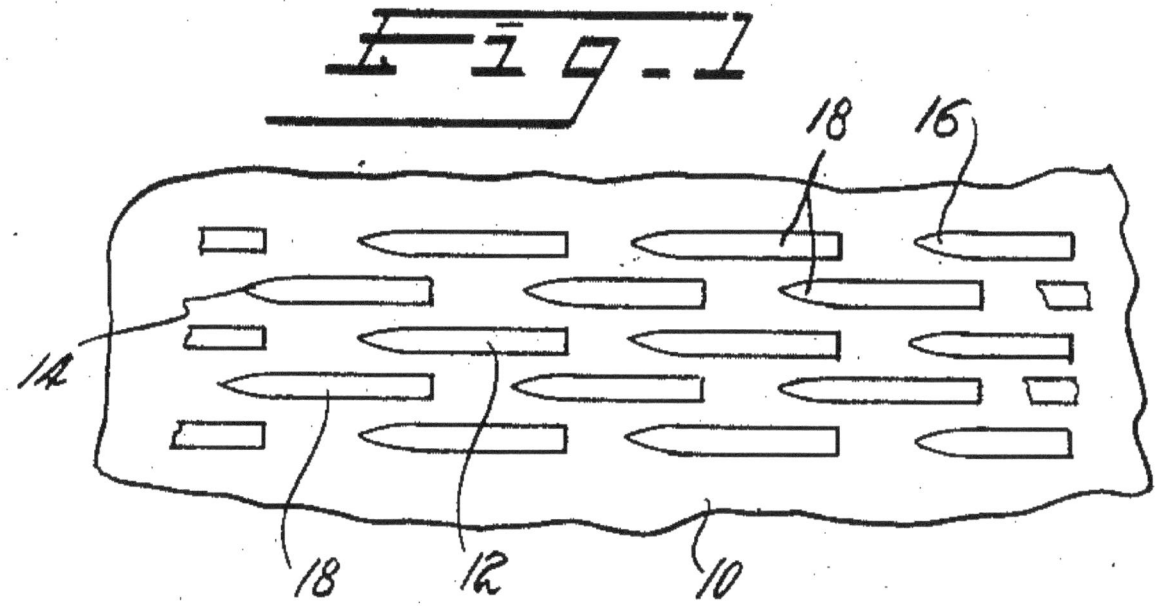

Fig. 87. Original "gang-nail" by Jureit. US Patent No. 2885749A filed 1955.

John Wesley Jureit, the other "Henry Ford" was another man influenced by World War Two prefabrication in the Pacific.[197] In 1949 he took on the first of two roles as the chief engineer in laboratories that tested building materials including trusses. In the first role, which was in a commercial laboratory, Jureit found he spent most of his time advising clients on how to improve their trusses rather than testing them. Despite the limitations of pre nailplated trusses he could see that that "builders were already warming up to the fact that trusses were the way to go. I could already see it was going to be a big industry. We just needed a better way to do it".[198] The "better way" came to him in a reflective moment in a church service[199] after he had gone into private practice in 1955. His idea which

---

[193] Maurer, Libby. Industry veterans Hark Back to Early Plates *in Structural Building Components Magazine*, November 2003. URL: http://www.sbcmag.info/article/2003/industry-veteran-hark-back-early-plates Date accessed: 5 August 2016.
[194] US Patent 2827676A.
[195] Plans are available at http://levittownbeyond.com/LevittownNJ.html. Date accessed: 5 August, 2016.
[196] Taylor, Peter. *Pers. Com.* May 11, 2016.
[197] Merullo. *Jureit ...* Pages not numbered.
[198] Jureit, J. Calvin quoted in Gang Nails Golden Anniversary, A visit with inventor Cal Jureit and his wife Marie in *Structural Building Componcnts Magazine* September/October 2005, 36.
[199] The legal arguments over the ownership of the patent that followed Jureit's lodgement were considerable due to his previous role in testing what would be competitors products so the origin of the idea away from work was something he stressed.

revolutionised the construction industry was the first nailplate that did not require supplementary nailing. The name "Gang-Nail" came soon after. This nailplate shown in Figure 87 had single straight teeth pressed from the plate which were long enough to secure the plate to the timber.

Many sawmills wanted to value add to their own wood and needed to set up at low cost but starting a truss plant in the beginning was not easy. The equipment needed to install plates simply did not exist or if they did exist the delivery times and cost precluded their use. Jureit became not just a plate manufacturer but also built the equipment to use them. He initially used a concrete vertical hydraulic press and steel table precision jigs to install them. The business was based on the razor blade principal – "give 'em the razors and they'll come back to you for blades"[200]

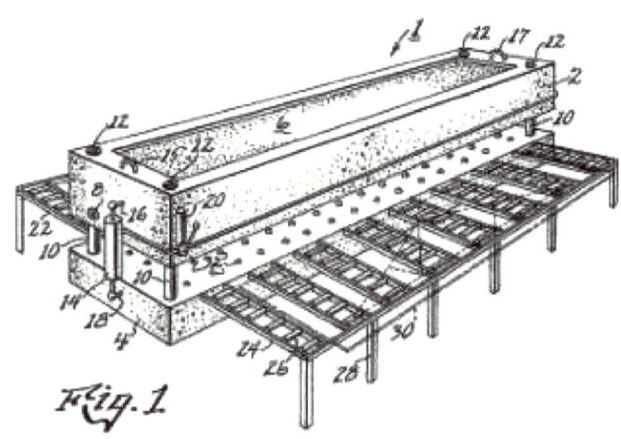

Fig. 88. Jureit's early vertical concrete press. US patent 3079607A.

Fig. 89. Historical nailplates.

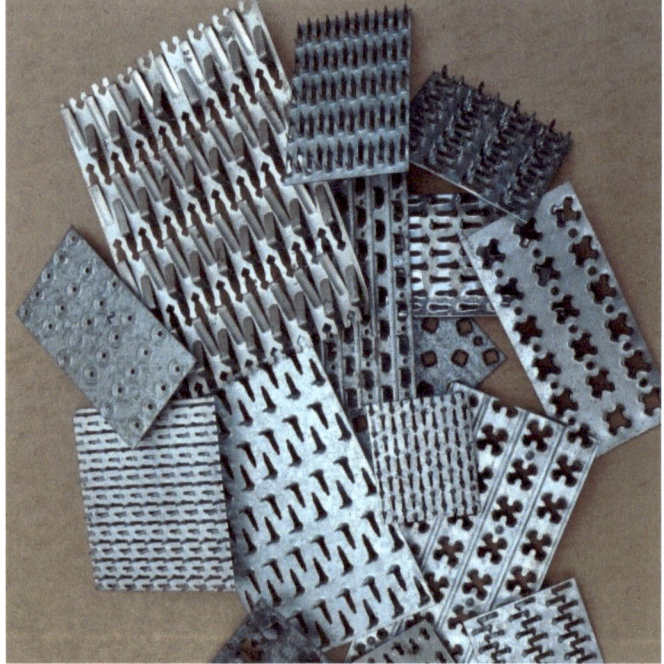

Fig. 90. Historical nailplates.

A period of litigation started over the ownership of Jureit's patent but while in place it allowed the Gang-Nail company[201] to have a dominant role in the early truss connector market. The argument of ownership in the end was academic as the validity of the patent was overturned.[202] This led to a plethora

---
[200] Jureit. *Visit ...*, 36.
[201] Later trading as Automated Building Components and eventually acquired by Mitek.
[202] Automated Building Components V. Hydro-Air Eng'g., (Eastern District of.Missouri. 1964) instigated in 1961.

of manufacturers with at one stage there being almost 30 manufacturers in the US alone, most of which no longer exist. Industry veterans in 2003 put the failure of so many companies to them being "content with their product, [and not recognising] the need to stay ahead of the curve like the front-runners. They lost a lot of ground by not constantly staying competitive and were eventually overshadowed by those who were willing to take up that challenge." Technical and economic pressures were driving changes to plate design and Jureit would ultimately have 60 related patents and Sandford would also continue to add innovations. On Juriet's death, his life work was summarised, "The whole notion about affordable housing and productivity increases came about because of his invention," said John A. White, former dean of engineering at the Georgia Institute of Technology. "Because of Henry Ford, cars evolved from being crafted one at a time to assembly-line construction, which made the automobile affordable. Jureit has been widely recognized for doing this for housing."[203] Jureit himself had a far more modest appraisal "You just scratch your head a little bit and think," he said. "It's not that hard."[204]

Fig. 91. Modern nailplate with multigrips connector.

The Jureit style nailplate had long single teeth at each punching and unlike the Sandford plate sheared the wood fibres which was later to cause problems with some softwood, for example Norwegian spruce, where the joint could fail in tension. In the softer timbers the "teeth had a tendency to compress the soft wood behind them with the result that the teeth force the formation of significantly larger openings or holes in the wood. The openings in the wood, in effect, spread or enlarge and permit the teeth to bend and slide from the openings." The tooth shape had to change.

Fig. 92. Platen type press.

Fig. 93. Roller type press

---

[203] Merullo. *Jureit* ... Pages not numbered.
[204] Merullo. *Jureit* ... Pages not numbered.

Economic forces from the pressures of automation would also force changes to tooth design. The roller press was invented by Sandford[205] but it would not roll either his own plate or that of Jureit with the straight teeth, both of which worked well on pattern presses. The twisted tooth plate was developed to allow instillation by rolling but also worked on the platen press. Fabrication was sped up to the extent that a truss could be produced within a minute.[206] One industry veteran commented that this "began the trend of creating automation first and a product to be used by that automation second."[207]

Truss adoption was hampered initially by the negative impression associated with early trusses as "houses with similar roofs lined streets for miles at a time because changing the truss manufacturing setup took time, effort, and therefore, money. Unfortunately, because of this brief period of time, the term pre-fabrication or "pre-fab" still carries a stigma."[208] Other factors complicating their adoption were

- Each manufacturer had their own testing methodology
- The need to work with Federal Housing Administration (FHA) and the many various local code jurisdictions in having their products and designs recognised led to persistent questions about structural adequacy.
- Each truss variation for each plate manufacturer had to be tested adding enormous cost on manufacturers and workload on the regulatory authorities.[209]

The Truss Plate Institute (TPI) was founded in the US in 1960 with Juriet and Sandford's companies as founding members. This organisation led to industry wide agreement on testing methods and truss design standards. The TPI still plays a critical role in the study and evaluation of new data as well as monitoring developments in the industry.

Gang-nails operation in Australia started during the 1962-65 international expansion of the business under the guidance of Jureit's brother Bill. By 1970, though the greatest uptake was in domestic housing there was industrial application as well. Perhaps caught up in the hype of the time, trusses of 200 ft (61 metres) were claimed to be practicable.[210]

---

[205] US patents 3212694A and 3435508A.
[206] US patent 3334579 A
[207] Vaccaro, Charlie quoted in Maurer, Libby. Industry veterans Hark Back to Early Plates in *Structural Building Components Magazine*, November 2003. URL: http://www.sbcmag.info/article/2003/industry-veteran-hark-back-early-plates Date accessed: 5 August 2016.
[208] MiTek. *History*. URL: https://www.mitek-us.com/about/History.aspx. Date accessed: 8 August 2016
[209] Truss plate Institute – history. URL: http://www.tpinst.org/history/ Date accessed: 8 August 2016
[210] Wallis, Norman. *Australian Timber Handbook* (Sydney: Angus and Robinson. 1970), 329. This length is possible in a bolted truss and "technically if you had large enough timber and could have a 10 lamination truss at 600crs a nailplated truss might be possible to span 60m."Smith. *Pers. Com* 19 August 2016.

Fig. 94. IBM1130 computer.

Trusses were initially designed using span tables which reduced the options available. If something more unusual or a girder truss was required this was designed from scratch by an engineer with a slide rule.[211] Computerisation which started in 1970 with the first truss software package, Auto-Truss, was developed by Gang-Nail and was offered on a time sharing basis to their customers the next year. This program was modified to run on an IBM 1130 computer[212] Computer aided design (CAD) was offered to the industry in 1970. In 1972, Gang-Nail's new program Auto Plot would prepare certified drawings which rapidly decreased the turnaround time for their customers. Gang nail would further develop software and released Auto Roof which produced the first framing plan. This software was still only available on a time sharing basis but in 1982 the Gang-Nail software was able to be run in house.[213] [214]

Computerisation has now developed to the point that files can be received directly from the CAD programs of the designer and loaded straight into the truss plants computer for quoting and design and so reducing the likelihood of error. One Australian plate manufacturer's computer program has a 30 metre limit to its design capacity but with everything over 16 metres still requiring an engineer to check the design. Trusses beyond 16 metres can be difficult to install and to brace and are beyond what would normally be supplied in domestic applications so in-house computing will deal with most day to day issues.

While it is possible to obtain a wide array of designs for the required project designed in house on the truss manufacturer's computer, at the beginning three truss types, the king post, Fink and Howe predominated which harked back to when trusses were designed more by intuition than science.[215] Now there are even more webbing possibilities but the most common truss type is the Fink which most people call an A-Type webbing (2 webs each side of apex) or B-Type webbing (4 webs each side of apex). For smaller spans (typically 4 m) a king post truss can be used, next (to 6 metres) would be queen post, then the A and B type Finks (9 and 13 metres respectively). Larger spans would more probably be a pitched Warren trusses. For exposed trusses, architects often prefer the Howe webbing profiles due to aesthetics.

---

[211] Smith, Matthew. *Pers. Com.* July 8, 2016.
[212] This computer gave many people their first interaction with computers and included inexpensive (for the time) removable disk storage.
[213] During the 1980's, the truss plant we were involved with briefly created their designs on a hand held calculator with a ribbon print out. These were faxed through to the plate manufacturer for checking. Something more complicated was designed by the plate manufacturer. Each month, the cost of the phone calls which were all long distance was at least equal to the wages of an employee!
[214] Structural Building Component Association. *Industry Timeline.* URL: http://www.sbcindustry.com/content/3/industry-timeline. Date Accessed: 9 August 2016.
[215] Truss Plate Institute. *Design Specifications for Light Metal Plate Connected Trusses TPI 60.* (Truss Plate Institute Inc: Miami. UD) Pages not numbered.

Stress graded timber was required for top and bottom cords in the US as early as 1960[216] and with the improved certainty about the structural properties of the timber being used and improved engineering and plate performance, timber sizes decreased from the standard 100x50 in the US as early as 1970. In Australia the normal size used is 90x35 with webs being 70x35. The truss has come a long way from the early empirically designed roofs of antiquity where bottom cords could be 500 mm deep! As early as 1970 it was said "light weight timber trusses of great strength and rigidity are beginning to replace the massive and complex structures normally associated with timber frames. Their rigidity eliminates sagging roof lines. Since all roof loads are transmitted through the external walls, interior partitioning can be of light construction, movable if desired. Interior foundations can be reduced or eliminated. Thus, overall economies can usually be achieved."[217]

Causes of Failure in Nailplated Trusses

Fig. 95. Incorrect storage of trusses. **Fig. 96.** Resultant failure of joint.

Failures of nailplated trusses do occur but they are rare. Some early failures were attributed to old formulation fire retardants that caused the timber to degrade over time[218] and issues were also reported from straight tooth plates but, overwhelmingly, then as now, problems are associated with on site storage and installation issues. One manufacturer reported, "Of all the failures I see 1% would be incorrect design (designer used the wrong roof weight, etc), 2% would be incorrect manufacture (wrong size or position of nailplate or wrong timber size or grade used), 95% would be poor erection. [poor erection issues were] mainly trusses out of plumb, installed in the wrong locations, not restrained correctly, boots not fixed off correctly, webs cut out by air conditioning installers, etc. 3% could be other issues like slab movement." [219]

---

[216] Truss Plate Institute. *Design ...,* Pages not numbered. Continuous lumber testing was available from at least 1959 and by 1974 technology was commercially available to detect the presence of rot.
[217] Wallis. *Australian ...,* 330.
[218] Emmick, Tim. *Metal Plated Wood Truss Failure Causes.* Penn State 2012. URL: https://failures.wikispaces.com/Wood+Truss+Failures#Metal%20Plated%20Wood%20Truss%20Failure%20Causes Date accessed: August 10, 2016.
[219] Smith, Matthew. *Pers. Com.* July 9, 2016.

Correct handling of trusses on site is critical and builders need to be well trained in their installation. Trusses can withstand very high vertical loads but are unstable when exposed to lateral loads until they are well braced. Because of this, installation requires great care so undue lateral stress is not imposed on the truss. Unless very small, trusses must never be lifted from one point. The installation requires the trusses to be installed straight and plumb with bracing and ties completed as they are being installed rather than waiting for all the trusses to be installed.

Fig. 97 Incorrect site storage

A variation of the nailplate is the knuckle Nailplate where the teeth are folded outwards much like a knuckle and are driven into the timber with a hammer instead of a press. They are secured into the timber differently from a normal plate as a "natural arc or dovetail effect is created by the nails as they penetrate into the timber. This provides positive resistance to nail withdrawal."[220] Their ease of installation site makes them suitable for a range of products such as shunt plates to dissipate electrical current on crossarms and in situ repairs. When labour costs are not an issue they can also be used to fabricate trusses.

Further Developments

Fig. 98. Nailplate has transformed from not just being the connector but being part of the structural member itself.

The nailplate was originally conceived as a means to speed up the fabrication of roof trusses but its versatility quickly saw it find application in other applications. In 1968 Carol Sandford patented the combination wood and metal truss intended for floor and flat roof trusses[221] known as the Steelwood where plate and brace are one item.

Other products that have been developed have been anti split products such as the pole-cat[222] and anti split plates for sleepers as well as reinforcement plates for bolts. One area that should have room for growth is using nailplates to upgrade lower F rated material by strengthening areas where there are natural features.

---

[220] Pryda. *Pryda Timber Connectors Nailplate Guide*. (Pryda: Dandenong South. 2012), 8.
[221] US Patent 3416283A.
[222] Invented by the author.

7. PRESSED METAL CONNECTORS

Corrugated galvanised iron sheet roofing was invented in the 1820's in England but this originally was made out of wrought iron which did not have the structural properties needed for high capacity pressed metal connectors. The 1890's saw wrought iron replaced with mild steel for sheeting, about the same time as steel stamping was introduced, but this did not immediately relate to the plethora of pressed metal connectors we now know. Some very basic connectors were developed including a joist hangers (patented 1895)[223] which has not changed in concept to modern days but they did not have sufficient impact to revolutionise timber construction. The role of TECO in the introduction of split ring connectors to the US and then on to Australia after World War One was discussed in the chapter relating to split rings and shear plates. The company was founded to "encourage the use of lumber in engineered construction, primarily through the development and sale of improved timber connectors."[224] Despite the charter to develop these improved connectors, there appeared to be a tardiness to develop a comprehensive range of pressed metal connectors once triple grips had been invented.

Pressed metal connectors would initially be called "secondary connections".[225] In the *Manual of Timber Connector Construction* by TECO in 1939, the only pressed metal connectors are clamping plates for railway sleepers[226] The first of these secondary connectors to make a large impression was the Trip-L-Grip, a trade name registered by TECO in 1946 for a connector for which a patent was lodged in 1944.[227] They are sold in Australia under the names Trip-L-Grip or triple grip and AS1684.2 refers to these as "framing anchors". It is reasonable to assume that the great need for prefabrication during the war drove its innovation and use. They were initially made in type A (left and right), the normal grip we know with the small leg bent inwards, Type B (left and right), with the same leg bent outwards and Type C with the leg not bent at all. Australian manufacturers generally only produce Type A now with the role of the Type B and C now being taken by the universal multi grip.

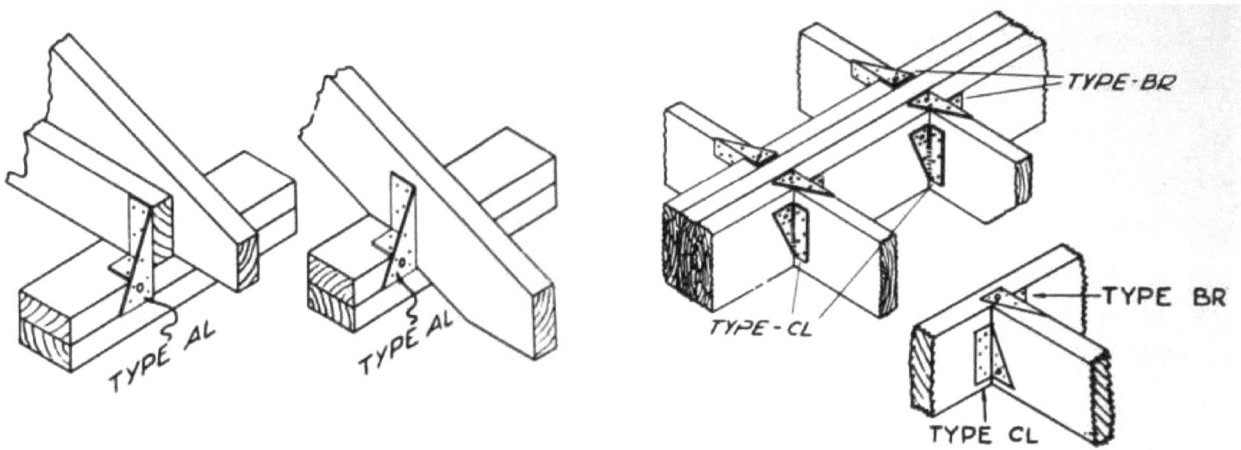

Fig. 99. Triple Grips.[228]

---

[223] US Patent 537505. This hanger used bar, not light pressed sheet, making them relatively expensive.
[224] Timber Engineering Company. *A Brief History of the Timber Engineering Company.* (No publication details 1958), pages not numbered.
[225] Timber Engineering Company. *Recreational ...*, 21.
[226] Timber Engineering Co. *Manual of Timber Engineering Construction.* (Washington: Timber Engineering Company, 1939), 2. Available https://archive.org/stream/ManualOfTimberConnectorConstruction/-TimberEngineeringCoCca35688#page/n1/mode/1up Date Accessed: 15 August 2016.
[227] US Patent 2413362A.
[228] Timber Engineering Company. *Specify Timber with the TECO System for industrial and Commercial Structures.* (Washington: Timber Engineering Company, 1950), 22.

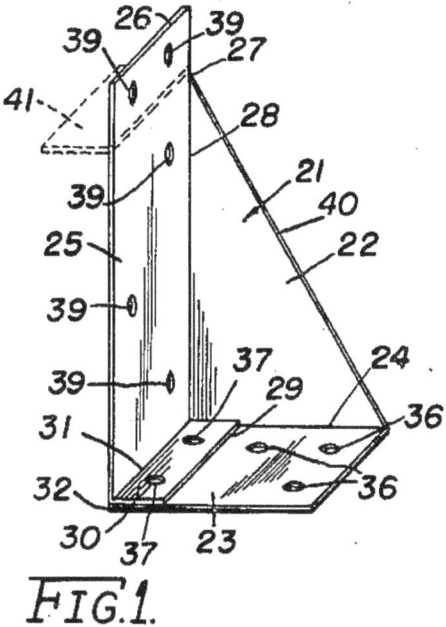

Fig. 100. A grip from 1940 which has minimal resistance to uplift.[229]

TECO claimed that these grips "provide the ideal connection for anchoring rafters to trusses or purlins, girts to columns, floor joists to beams, ceiling joists to beams or trusses, beams to posts and ceiling joists to small headers. Wind anchorage is always a factor with these anchors, rafters are tied tight – a strong guard against uplifting of roofs. For earthquake areas, Trip-L-Grips are always useful in knitting the entire structure into a better shock absorbing unit."[230] Despite alternatives now being available, this grip is still the mainstay for attaching trusses to wall frames[231] which is not surprising as it is a very elegant design. The triple grip's angular shape is intended "to resist shear stresses [by affording] short lever arms for the stresses introduced in to the clip by eccentricities. [As well] ... the stresses introduced into the clips are uniformly distributed throughout the cross section of the metal and in no case do the stresses converge or concentrate at one point which would cause a point or zone of weakness." Irrespective of the forces applied the interlocking nails ensure that some are always in shear preventing the withdrawal of the nails and so dislodging of the bracket.[232] An even more effective method of nailing called "double shear" would later be patented by Simpson Strong-Tie.

Although pressed metal joist hangers were available by 1958, TECO had only one extra secondary connector added to their range, a Du-al-Grip, a triple grip alternative for lighter structures.[233] This is basically the same product that is sold in Australia under the trade name Unitie or similar. In 1970, Automated Building Components (Aust.) Pty. Ltd. which produced the Gang-Nail product purchased a controlling interest in the Australian company Timber Engineering Company Pty. Ltd. (TECO) which produced a number of timber connectors, some of which were manufactured under license to TECO Washington, U.S.A. TECO (Australia) became a fully owned subsidiary of A.B.C. (Aust.) Pty. Ltd. in 1973.[234] So, between 1958 and 1970 what happened? And the answer, apparently, is "Not a great deal." The patent on the triple grip expired in 1964 which allowed other manufacturers into the market but it did not result in the profusion of connectors we see today.

---

[229] US Patent 2321221A.
[230] Timber Engineering Company. *Recreational ...*, 21.
[231] Smith, Matthew. *Pers. Com.* 16 August 2016.
[232] US Patent 2413362A.
[233] Timber Engineering Company. *A Brief History of the Timber Engineering Company.* (No publication details 1958), 2.
[234] Mitek. *History* URL: http://www.mitek.com.au/About/OurHistory.aspx. Date Accessed: 17 August 2016

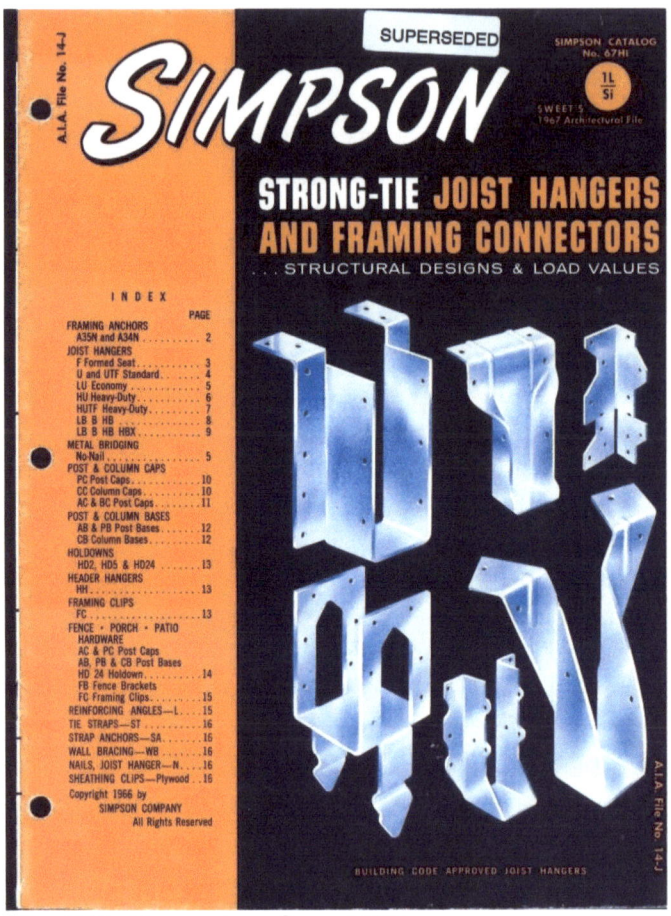

Fig. 101. Connectors from 1967

The revolution in connectors was probably initiated in 1982 when Simpson Strong-Tie was independently approached by two industry leaders in the US to address concerns about the available connectors. Emerging from this was the Truss Hanger Adjustable (THA) which "was intended to fulfil a great number of needs with just 2 or 3 stock keeping units (skus). There was the single 2x [50 mm] width, a double 2x width and a 4x [100 mm] width to accommodate parallel chord 4x2 [100x50 mm] trusses in the initial offering back in the early '80s. The design used slant nailing through the hanger bucket flange through the carried truss at an angle into the header (supporting) truss. Today we call that 'double shear nailing'.[235] It was an attempt, early on, to provide the truss industry with an adjustable hanger that would fit on 2x6 [150x50] thru 2x12 [300x50] common truss girder bottom chords. Back in that era, the truss plants were delighted to be able to stock so few skus and accomplish the vast majority of their truss-to-truss connection needs. The modern THA Series (with 11 skus) is still a mainstay at many truss plants across North America."[236] At this stage Simpson Strong-Tie have more than double the number of connectors than their competitors and have the largest number of patented connectors in the industry.

When asked what is driving this explosion of connectors from one company, Stan Sias of Simpson Strong-Tie advised that many of the connectors in their catalogues "were in fact request from customers, specifiers (architects, engineers, building designers and DIYers) and code enforcement officials over the years. Much has been done to simplify installation and inspection. Some market development comes from listening and reacting proactively to those involved with code enforcement and standards development. Other market development comes from alternative building methodologies. There is much to be learned from observing cold formed steel, masonry and timber construction. We can look at some existing parts and see ways to increase their loads utilising different fasteners (screws to replace nails let's say). Then there are the constant misinstallations that need to be sorted out and simplified.

All of this is done to exceed customer satisfaction and grow specifier confidence. With education comes expectations. As we learn more from post incident (hurricanes, tornadoes, floods, snow) inspections, and sharing those findings with the world, we often find minimal ways to make maximum impact on building durability during these events. …. In North America, we have many regional building techniques or methodologies that may require differing connectivity. Some areas are controlled by wind or snow whereas others may be controlled by seismic activity. As we learn more about design and durability we develop connectors/fasteners to make the process more user/inspector/specifier

---

[235] US Patent 4480941 A, files March 4, 1983.
[236] Sias, Stan. *Pers Com.* Sept 7, 2016.

friendly."[237] Herb Kuhn[238] advised that the challenges for the future for all connector manufacturers will include designing for ever increasing wind loads and finding ways of retrofitting pre-BCA compliant homes.

One ongoing concern with pressed metal connectors has been the incorrect use of fasteners and fasteners are generally the limiting factor with the bracket. After Cyclone Tracy which devastated the northern Australian capital Darwin, engineered houses fared worse than those built using traditional methods. There were many reasons for this, not the least being an inadequate understanding of the forces that were in play during a cyclone of this magnitude. But another reason was builders failing to install the connectors in accordance with the manufacturers' recommendation. I recall seeing an image of a failed roof truss connection where there were only three nails in total used on the triple grip whereas ten should have been used. It was practices such as this that have led to a rigorous multi stage inspection regime under the Building Code of Australia.

When I first started selling triple grips in the 1980's there were still issues with builders using clout nails instead of the required but more expensive connector nails. The heads of clouts could become brittle and break off even during driving[239] and were a slightly thinner diameter. While warning about their use persists, the issue now causing concern is the use of gun driven hardened nails. The practice is common in the US which uses "positive placement" nail guns which allow the operator to locate the nail hole exactly before driving the nail. In Australia, the practice was to use a less expensive finishing gun and nail through the metal and the results rarely[240] met manufacturers' guidelines with smaller connectors such as triple grips and multi grips.[241] The necessary clearances were difficult to achieve. For example, 3 mm from any edge or hole and spaced evenly apart, and also the nails could be over driven.

Fig. 102. Poorly installed grip using gun nails.

In 2015 there was a crackdown on the practice, in Queensland at least, of gun nailing triple grips and multi grips and, if their use is observed, "the QBCC [Queensland Building and Construction Commission] will deem the work defective and require immediate remedial works to be undertaken to remedy the situation."[242] The QBCC in consultation with manufacturers and Timber Queensland had a real concern that the continued inappropriate "use of gun nailing tie-down connectors may lead to catastrophic failures of roof structures in high-wind events".[243] Gun nails can be used with products such as straps, cyclone ties and joist hangars as there is more room for the nail and the necessary clearances can be achieved. The QBCC identified "issues such as inadequately-sized nails, inadequate edge distances and close groupings of nail fixings leave

---

[237] Sias, Stan. *Pers Com.* Sept 7, 2016.
[238] Kuhn, Herb. *Pers. Com.* October 7, 2016. Herb is managing Director of Simpson Strong-tie Australia.
[239] Gang Nail. *Gang Nail News* Issue No 21, October 1996, 1.
[240] Smith, Matthew. *Pers. Com.* 5 October 2016. Similarly Mitek GN Guidelines 182 August 2012. Mitek identified problems with gun nail fixing in 2000 in their GN Guidelines 33 and the practice persisted till 2015 in Queensland!!
[241] Refer to Gang-Nail Guidelines 33 and 182 for a number of images showing incorrectly gun nail installed connectors.
[242] Queensland Building and Construction Commission. *Gun Nailing of Framing Anchors and Straps*. URL: https://www.qbcc.qld.gov.au/blog/tradie-talk/gun-nailing-framing-anchors-straps Date accessed: 4 October 2016.
[243] Queensland. *Gun ...,*

tradespeople with little chance of providing compliant connections." Now, some connecters are being made without holes specifically to suit gun nails. One American manufacturer MiTek TECO has developed nails for use with positive placement guns that are colour coded for length and head stamped for diameter making for easy inspection. It would be expected that something similar will be available in Australia in coming years to overcome the valid concerns of manufacturers and regulatory bodies.

Inappropriate Use of Metal Connectors

Fig. 103. Broken Triple grips in boardwalk subject to wave action.

Fig. 104. Failure of Boardwalk during flood fastened with multigrips.

While the use of metal connectors has been very successful I have observed their application in boardwalks where they have not been satisfactory. Arguably these were applications for which the connector was not intended. Figure 103 shows stainless multigrips which, while being a quality product, was not an appropriate product and the irregular action of waves has caused the grips to fail. In Figure 104 triple grips were too light to handle flood forces. Another problem observed is the connection of the 150x75 mm hardwood joists to the headstocks with grips is not strong enough to hold the end of the joists should they need to be straightened. These are applications outside of the intended use of the product. The best connection in this application is a more robust bolt or fabricated angle.

With incremental improvements to the design of pressed metal connectors and better installation we can only expect that the future of pressed metal connectors will only increase in importance over the coming years.

8. RELATION OF F RATING TO JOINT GROUP

The correct fastener design is very much dependent on the joint group of the timber which will also be nominated with an F grade. Is there a connection between the two? I have written in detail about the determining the F grades of hardwood in my book *Grading Hardwood – Understanding AS2082*. The same principles apply when grading pine and cypress. The determination of an F grade is a combination of the strength of the species as determined by testing samples that are absolutely free of any defect then modifying that by the impact of a defect in the piece being graded.

Structural Grade	1	2	3	4
% of solid strength	75	60	50	40
Species	Mountain Ash	Rose Gum	Spotted gum	Bl Ironbark
F grade	F14	F14	F14	F14
Joint group	J3, JD3	J3, JD2	J1, JD1	J1, JD1

Table 7. Relationship of F grade to defect size.

Table Seven shows that, if the timber's only specification is F14, it can be supplied as a piece of virtually defect free but low durability mountain ash or just as legitimately it could be high durability broad leaf ironbark but of exceptionally low quality. The appearance of Structural Grade 4 is so poor that people would not generally accept it.[244] The visual difference between the two pieces is size of the defect which can occur anywhere in the length of the timber.

Fig. 105. Bolts in close proximity on new crossarm.

Fig. 106. Crossarm that was replaced

The designer should be aware that the placement of a defect can be critical to the success of a joint. Figure 105 shows a new 100x100 mm crossarm fitted to a powerpole and in the red circle there is a horizontal brace bolt (14 mm hole) and an insulator pin (22 mm hole) both in very close proximity. The following image shows the arm that was replaced where the close proximity of the holes contributed to a failure. This piece of timber had no defect at that point but had there been a 25 mm unsound knot – which would have produced F17 in spotted gum or a 33 mm knot in ironbark, again producing F17 had been combined with these two bolts failure would have been certain much earlier.

It was not accidental that there was no defect at this location as the power authority involved was very aware of the risk and their crossarm specification required those areas that had fasteners to be defect free. Likewise, the designer needs to consider if his joints are going to carry a high load and

---

[244] I say "generally" as there was a group who would. The grade was often referred to as "hippie grade".

specify where the defect size should be limited. For instance, hardwood graded to Structural Grade 2 (producing F17 in unseasoned spotted gum and F22 in broad leaf ironbark) will allow 150x100 mm rot pockets that are 3 mm deep every per 2.0 m length. This is not ideal material into which to insert a nailplate.

Unseasoned Timber						
Joint Group	J1	J2	J3	J4	J5	J6
Basic density kg/m^3	750	600	475	380	300	240
Seasoned Timber						
Joint Group	JD1	JD2	JD3	JD4	SD5	JD6
Air-dry density at 12%	940	750	600	475	380	300
Table 8. Density/joint group relationship.[245]						

The joint group is related not to the strength of the timber but its density in kg per m^3 which is basically the amount of wood fibre available at the joint. The values for unseasoned timber are deceptively low until it is understood that they are based on "basic density", a measurement not often used in the building related professions but normal in the paper industry. Basic density is the mass of an oven dried specimen divided by its volume when unseasoned. The terminology "air-dry" used for measuring the density of seasoned timber, in technical publications, includes kiln drying.

So to summarise, there is no direct connection between F grades and Joint groups but the choice of the wrong F grade can complicate joint design by permitting a defect where it may be inappropriate. Consideration should be given to whether limits should be placed on the position of natural feature.

---

[245] National Association of Forest Industries *Timber Manual Datafile P1 – Timber Species and Properties.* (NAFI), 7

9. WEATHER EXPOSED JOINTS

The large majority of joints are protected from the weather meaning that, while ever they are protected and no moisture enters the joint, there is no reason for any degrade. As the European experience shows, it would be reasonable to talk in hundreds of years life, not in decades for an expected life. But this is not the case once the joint is exposed to the weather. Considerable attention has to be given to the joint to counter the effects of moisture, and additionally in the Australian environment, UV so an acceptable life can be achieved. This chapter will give practical advice on how to detail a weather exposed joint by looking at handrails, probably the most commonly experienced application most builders will encounter.

Fig. 107. Top rail after 30 years in Gatton, Queensland.

Fig. 108. Moisture shedding rail.

Unlike internal joints, the species selection is the first and most vital decision. Untreated pine will perform well inside a house so long as it is protected from termites but, when weather exposed, the normal consideration would be to use hardwood. Even then only a few species perform well. These species include spotted gum, ironbark, tallowwood, grey gum and Gympie messmate and were known under the term "royal species". In 1986, the author supplied one of his first bridges to a park opposite his home giving him the opportunity to watch it closely over the years. The first noticeable effect of weathering was that the tops of 45 mm wide rails (supplied in select quality spotted gum) eventually started to degrade. Figure 107 is typical of the degrade that occurred after 29 years but some areas had more degrade. (The rails were actually replaced a week after the image was taken but could have just been rolled over and the protected edge placed upwards). Observing this degrade led the author to change the design of the rails he produced so that they all shed moisture. Refer Figure 108 for an example of an ex 50 mm vertical rail.

Fig. 109. Diagonally aligned top rail on heritage listed fence.

Fig. 110. Footbridge with diagonally aligned top rail.

The most effective water shedding railing is when the top rail is mounted on the diagonal. The image on the left is from a heritage listed cricket ground at the Gatton campus of the University of Queensland. The image was taken in 2014 just before it was replaced. Some rails had failed but most are still sound. It probably should have been replaced ten years earlier. The fence is known to predate 1940 but by how much is not known. This gives a useful life of at least 65 years. Taking positive steps to shed moisture will reward you.

Attaching the Top Rail to the Post

Fig. 111. Top rail in Canberra fastened from underneath.

Fig. 112. Same structure where the top rail was extended and fastened from the top.

TIMBER JOINTS

Fig. 113. Decay at top rail join.

As for the need for fastening from underneath, The decay in Figure 113 clearly illustrates the shortcomings of top fixing. The main part of the top rail in that structure is fastened from underneath using galvanised brackets and is in good order despite having some age. An extension which was top fixed has failed. It is not hard to fix from underneath and, like a moisture shedding profile, well worth the extra effort involved.

The top rail in the same structure is flat and is not shedding moisture quickly. This is allowing any moisture to more readily go down the join and enter through the end grain (which can absorb moisture 8 times faster than through the face) and cause decay at the ends. There should be at least 6 mm end clearance between the rails to prevent moisture being held by capillary action but this constitutes a possible finger entrapment. A strap over the join was the old way of protecting the join from moisture and is still good practice (see Figure 109). The strap prevents finger entrapment as well if a gap is introduced.

Spans

Fig. 114. Each top rail has taken a set downwards.

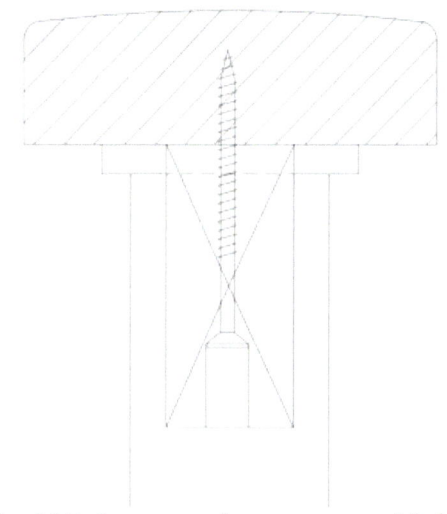

Fig. 115. Later versions use a multiple span with a stiffener underneath.

A structurally sound joint will not keep timber straight which, particularly when weather exposed, will tend to move. The condition of the top rail timber in Figure 114 was excellent but what distracts from the aesthetics is that every piece had taken a set downwards. This was despite the top rail being ex 125x100 mm with a water shedding profile, and the span only being 2400 mm! This unfortunate situation occurred soon after the boardwalk was completed. When I look at the image above and reflect on what my eye saw on site, it appeared much worse on location. The visual effect is compounded as it is an unbroken line and the eye tends to magnify the effect of the set.

Instead of the original heavy size which is expensive and difficult to produce in long lengths, a horizontal top rail (ex 150x50 mm) with a domed top extending over two spans would have been better. It would then require a 100x50 mm on edge underneath as a stiffener. This has proved stable. Whatever design option you choose, the important thing is to not have simple spans. Instead, support the top rail over three posts as mentioned. Using 2000 mm as the normal post spacing for larger size rails means that a multiple span can be sourced from a readily available[246] 4200 mm length. As invariably happens, the run is not a multiple of 4000 mm and if needed you can source a single 6000 mm length to finish without too many problems. Alternatively, a centre prop can be used if lengths are single span.

Fig. 116. Breaking the line of sight with a post.

Attaching the Post to the joist.

The complication in attaching the post to the structure is shrinkage. If, for example, you use a 75 mm thick unseasoned beam and a 125x125 mm post the total thickness is 200 mm. If you have specified a lower shrinkage timber like spotted gum with 6% movement you have to deal with 11-12 mm of shrinkage. It will also take about 4 to 5 years for the timber to stabilise. No one wants to return initially after six months and then annually for the next four years to tighten the nuts. You cannot specify kiln dried as it is impossible to commercially dry anything beyond 50 mm thick[247] and recycled is likely to behave just like green off saw timber.

Fig. 117. Volute washer on post.

As was mentioned in the section on threaded fasteners, a product that has long been used in the power industry for pole hardware that is impractical to retighten is a volute washer[248]. These stainless steel coils can take up 25 mm of shrinkage without the need to ever retighten. These should be an integral part of any railing post attachment. Figure 117 shows its application on a post. A square washer is required under the nut and, if going against a painted surface, our practice is to use a square washer underneath as well. Ideally, the post should be separated from the girder by a spacer about 6 mm thick. This will minimise the contact between the two members and reduce the likelihood of moisture being retained – refer Figure 118..

---

[246] Readily available, that is, in sizes such as 150x50 mm, not readily available in 125x100 mm which has to be very straight to pass through the planer.

[247] This fact is not widely recognised and sizes of 150x150 mm and 200x200 mm are frequently specified as kiln dried.

[248] The volute washer is a coil of approximately 6 mm stainless spring steel wire that compresses within itself. It is available in a range of sizes to suit 12, 16, 20 and 24 mm bolts. The volute washer needs a square washer under the nut. When we use them on a painted surface we use a large square washer under the volute washer itself to prevent damage to the paint. With the brand we use, the m12/16 washer measures approx. 65 mm across and about 30 mm high and the m20/24 washer measures 85x35 mm. Remember that you need longer bolts. In the image the washer is not fully tightened so it can be seen.

Fig. 118. Decay in tropical zone because of direct contact.

Fig 119. Split post because screws are in a straight line.

Just as it is important to stagger the screw-lines on decking it is equally important to do so on any joint where the screws are aligned with the grain direction. Aim for a minimum of 16 mm stagger. See Figure 119 which shows damage to a post due to screws in a straight line.. It is important to predrill the full depth and, where a coach screw is used, do two stage drilling to give clearance for the unthreaded portion under the head.

It is not uncommon to see handrails incorporating nailplates, particularly in timber bridges, where the handrail is a structural component supporting the whole. Invariably, the effect of wetting and drying forces the nailplate from the timber once the plate has withdrawn 2-3 mm the connection value is reduced by 50%. While these allow very economical construction they should not be used.

Fig. 120. Nailplate in handrail being forced out.

Fig. 121. A well detailed handrail that avoids the issues that can prematurely degrade handrails.

Figure 121 which shows a handrail at the Cairns marina in North Queensland shows how it is possible to attend to all these details in design and at the same time deliver exceptional aesthetics (albeit with a stainless post, not timber).

So, by careful attention to small points of detail to a weather exposed joint, a significantly longer life can be achieved with minimal impact on cost and a vast reduction in maintenance cost.

10. JOINTS IN GLUED BEAMS AND PANELS

Two relatively new timber products, laminated beams and cross laminated timber have led to the development of, if not new joints, at least improvements in existing technology. The best known of these two new products is laminated beams (called gluelam in the industry). Laminating timber is not a new idea. Bolt laminated timber bridges using unseasoned timber were known from 1838 in the UK and followed in Australia in the 1850's.[249] These bridges, in South Australia at least, had a relatively long life of 40 years and were very inexpensive to build compared to steel but required a lot of maintenance and so were not seen as a long term answer. Buildings using glue laminated beams from seasoned timber are also known in the UK from the 1840's and some are still in service because they are not exposed to the weather. But these early examples, using moisture prone animal glues are more curiosities than serious production products. The first patent for a horizontal laminated beam was granted to Otto Hetzer in Germany 1909.[250]

Fig. 122. Hardwood gluelam at National Arboretum, Canberra.

The technology came to the US in 1934 through an associate of Otto Hetzer and, in 1942, water resistant phenol-resorcinol adhesive was introduced. The first commercial standard for laminated beams was only introduced in 1963 in the US. Laminated beam production in Australia predates the establishment of dedicated laminated beam plants. Prior to these commercial plants, the war saw storage buildings with 30 m spans constructed from gluelam.[251] One Australian manufacturer, Hyne has been making beams since the 1960's and it is believed that plants existed in the early 1950's.[252] In some overseas countries, where their manufacture is highly automated, the price is less than one third of that in Australia[253] meaning the market for laminated beams is large. Because Australian beams are still fabricated using labour intensive methods, the price is depressing the potential market. Australian costs for a basic GL17 untreated beam vary from roughly $3600 for the smaller beams to $4000 for the larger sizes. The largest size listed by the Glue Laminated Timber Association, 660x135 mm is also much smaller than that which is available overseas.

---

[249] Glencross-Grant, Rex, Ian Berger. The European Influence on Laminated Timber Arch Road Bridges in Colonial Australia, 1852-90 In *World Congress On Timber Engineering 2016*. 3067-8.
[250] Glued Laminated Timber association . *Gluelam – Performance Record*. URL: http://www.glulam.co.uk/performance History.htm. date accessed: 2 January 2017.
[251] Nolan. *Forgotten ...*, xxii.
[252] Mansell, Robert. *Pers. Com.* 5 January 2017.
[253] "The approx. price for a 90 x 450mm European Whitewood (Spruce) straight glulam beam is GBP 720 per cbm. The majority of glulam used in the UK is imported from Scandinavia, Denmark, Germany and Austria. Generally depends on whether the glulam beams are standard cross sections and straight beams. Bespoke beams and curved sections are generally imported from Scandinavia & Denmark and occasionally Austria." Gomm, Paul. *Pers. Com.* 9 January 2017. Paul is with Technical Timber services Lt in the UK. The exchange rate at time of writing $1Au = £0.57.

The very large sizes that are possible and the fact that the timber was seasoned meant that they initially suited construction using splitrings and shear plates. Quickly, alternate methods of fixings suited specifically for laminated beams were developed. These include timber rivets, epoxy bonded bolts, and precision hardware that in some sense replicates the effect of traditional joints. Modern CNC processing of straight precision machined and dimensionally stable timber even allows for millimetre perfect craftsman joints of earlier times.

Fig. 123. Timber rivet.

Fig. 124. Typical riveted connection.

Timber rivets are not common in the Australian market but are an established part of timber construction in the US and Canada and has been included in the US's National Design Specification for Wood Construction since 1997.[254] Timber rivets are a highly developed form of nail that make single shear steel to wood splice joints. They are normally installed through metal side plates with air guns. The timber is not predrilled. Their simplicity and speed of installation can make them cost effective against bolts and shear plate construction. But, apart from economics, there are distinct structural advantages in using them. Connecting large beams with a few large bolts cause "large localised stresses and force brittle ruptures in timber"[255] but small diameter fasteners, providing there are sufficient quantity, will achieve the same effect without localising forces. This is a great advantage especially where high wind or earthquakes are expected. Because no timber is removed with predrilling or housing joints, the designer is able to utilise the full cross section of the member which can reduce the member size.[256] As mentioned in the discussion of F grades and joint types, the presence of timber defects can affect the joint. With timber rivets this is greatly diminished.

---

[254] Williams. *Timber ...*, 27.
[255] Zarnani, Pouyan, Pierre Quenneville. *Timber Rivet Connection*. (Melbourne: Forest and Wood Products Australia, 2016), 5.
[256] Williams, Christopher. Timber Rivets in *Structure Magazine* March 2006, 26-7. URL: http://www.structuremag.org/wp-content/uploads/2014/09/SF-Timber-Rivets-March-061.pdf. Date accessed: 2 January 2017.

The nails, available in 90, 65 and 40 mm lengths[257] have a wide flat face with two rounded edges (similar to the cut nail Type A in Figure 28) and measure 6.4 mm by 3.18 mm with a tapered head 6.4 mm long spreading to 8.7 mm at the top. The nail is driven through the plate and the heads are left protruding 3.2mm. The nail deforms in the hole and wedges tightly in the 6.9 mm round holes in the side plate.

Fig. 125. Studs epoxied into laminated beam.

The use of steel rods epoxied into glulams to achieve connections started in Denmark in about 1980[258] and were seen as offering better aesthetics due to the lack of plates and more design freedom. Distinct added advantages are that the bolt is protected from atmospheric corrosion and, providing the member is large enough, fire. As a joint, it is prone to longitudinal splitting caused by shear forces acting on the steel rods so the challenge is "develop a high strength moment-resisting connection having reliable shear strength and significant ductility that could perform well in seismic conditions".[259] This required a joint with a large reserve of capacity which is not desirable with very expensive material though the likelihood of longitudinal splitting may be reduced by also epoxying in transverse bolts.[260]

Unlike the timber rivet which can be installed on site by relatively unskilled workers, this approach has led to "inadequately mixed and incorrectly applied epoxy" and, as the work cannot be visually checked, it is recommended that the bolts be installed in a factory setting by skilled personnel.[261] The correct choice of epoxy is also critical and one researcher advised that the "best results have been achieved by using a low viscosity epoxy that can flow around the embedded rod ensuring full encapsulation".[262] Because the epoxy is stronger than the timber, like the rivet, there is no need to factor in the timber that has been removed.

The process involves drilling a hole about 6 mm larger than the dowel and then centralising the bar in the centre of the hole and the end is sealed . Epoxy is injected into the base of the hole until it flows out a hole at the other end. The bolts are situated at the top and the bottom of the beam for compression and tension loads. By using mild steel reinforcing bars the required ductility can be achieved. The bolt arrangement varies considerably. Figure 125 shows short studs protruding past the end of the beam which are intended to marry into a metal bracket. Other arrangements can include terminating in coupling nuts set flush with the end of beam and, alternatively, with long rods extending which are epoxied into the matching laminated beam.

---

[257] A prudent designer would ensure only one nail length is used throughout to ensure there are no errors during fabrication.
[258] Moss, Peter J1 , Andrew Buchanan, Ka Wong. *Moment-Resisting Connections in Glulam Beams*. Pages not numbered. URL: http://timber.ce.wsu.edu/Resources/papers/9-4-1.pdf . Date accessed: 3 January 2017.
[259] Moss. *Moment ...,* pages not numbered.
[260] Moss. *Moment ...,* pages not numbered
[261] Batchelar, Mark, Ken McIntosh. Structural Joints in Glulam.*New Zealand Timber Design Journal* Issue 4, Volume 7, 18. URL: http://www.timberdesign.org.nz/files/Structural%20Joints%20In%20Glulam.pdf. Date accessed: 3 January 2017.
[262] Batchelar. *Structural ...,* 18.

Fig. 126. Concealed aluminium bracket.   **Fig. 127.** Concealed hook connector.

Heavy connectors such as timber rivets and bolted connections can be very effective but are also very visible. The same can be said for light but effective metal connectors such as joist hangars. The exposed joints are also subject to fire damage The best aesthetics and the best fire resistance is achieved when the joint is not visible. Over the last 20 years there has been considerable research and innovation aimed to producing new products, both in the fittings and the associated fixings.

The two images in Figures 126 and 127 only hint at the wide variety of components that is available to suit many of the timber jointing requirements that might be met. In one way they are a revisiting and perfecting of old traditional joints which incorporated dowels and mortice and tenons. The Italian manufacturer, Rothoblaas, is probably the market leader for this style of product in Australia.

Cross laminated timber, known in Australia as CLT or in Europe as solid wood panel (SWT), was initially developed in Switzerland in the 1970's as a development of the plywood industry. CLT utilising sawn, not veneer stock, emerged in Europe in the early 1990's and its uptake was driven by the green building movement, better efficiencies in production and favourable building code changes in some jurisdictions".[263] Despite looking like "jumbo" plywood it is different in that alternate layers are at 90 degrees to the previous layer which gives greater dimensional stability to the panels. This cross lamination provides relatively high strength and stiffness properties in both directions causing it to act in a similar manner to a reinforced concrete slab but with only one fifth of the weight.[264] The arrangement of the laminations gives increased resistance to splitting and better connections. Like laminated beams their size is limited only by the factory and what can physically be carted and beams up to 500 mm thick, 18 m long and 3.0m high are known.[265] Because of their large size, the impact of defect in the individual laminates is limited so material that has failed MPG grading can potentially be used in their production.

---

[263] Timber Development Association. *Massive Timber construction Systems Cross Laminated timber (CLT)*. (Melbourne: Forest and Wood Products Association, 2015), 6.
[264] Timber Development Association. *Massive ...*, 5,6.
[265] Mohammad ,M., Sylvain Gagnon, Bradford K. Douglas, Lisa Podesto. *Introduction to Cross Laminated Timber*, 4. URL http://www.forestprod.org/buy_publications/resources/untitled/summer2012/Volume%2022,%20Issue%202%20Mohammad.pdf. Date accessed: 6 January 2017.

Fig. 128. First CLT office building in Australia using 2000 m3 of CLT[266]

CLT buildings have started being built in southern states, the first being the Docklands Library and Community Centre. At the time of writing there is no production facility for CLT in Australia so the product that is used is imported from Europe. The systems that have been developed have proved successful for temperate climates and in 2016, a multimillion dollar research project was started in Queensland with the aim of extending it to tropical and subtropical climates.

With a new product has come the need for new connections. There have been three approaches:

- Carpentry, by the use of CNC technology to make interlocking profiles
- Traditional Fasteners, using products such as nails, screws, bolts and brackets
- Innovative or proprietary items.

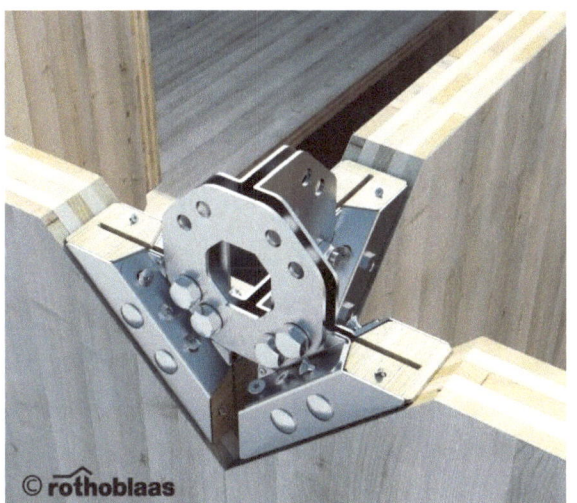
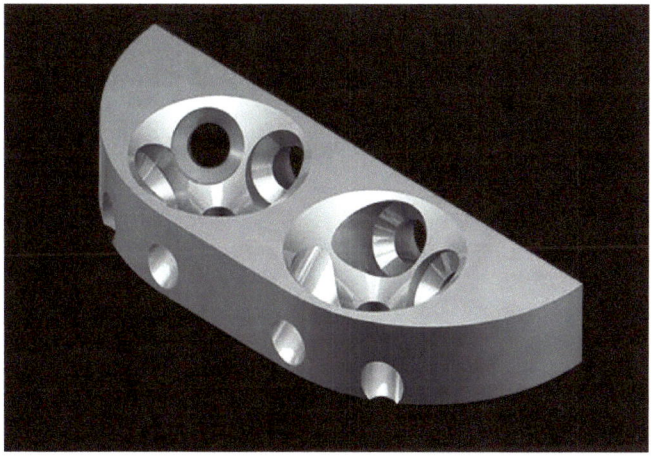

Fig. 129. Innovative CLT fixing bracket by Rothoblaas. **Fig. 130**. innovative CLT fixing by Sherpa.

---

[266] Stora Enso Australia's first wooden office built with Stora Enso CLT. Http: http://buildingandliving.storaenso.com/news/news-and-press-releases/ustralia-office-tora-nso- Date Accessed: 6 January 2017.

Unlike normal construction where plywood might be part of a structural panel, CLT is the panel itself so this brings extra considerations beyond the strength and stiffness characteristics of the joint. Other factors that have to be considered are performance under fire, air tightness, sound insulation, durability and vibration. This can involve the introduction of membranes where the walls meet the floor and even under the brackets.[267] Because timber will shrink and swell as the environment changes, the connections also have to take this into consideration.[268]

While there is nothing precluding their use, the application of rivets is rare. Likewise, bearing type fasteners such as split rings and shear plates and toothed connectors could be used but it is expected that these will be limited to applications where there is a high load.[269] A range of proprietary products has been developed include screws from 4 to 14 mm in diameter but up to 1500 mm long[270] that do not require predrilling in most cases. Epoxied systems similar to those used in laminated beams have also been utilised. Also available is a wide range of very innovative fixings such as those illustrated in Figures 129 and 130. With such a new product with such vast potential it is reasonable to expect that further innovation will continue over coming years.

---

[267] Karacabeyli, Errol, Brad Douglas, Editors. *CLT Handbook: Cross Laminated Timber US Edition*. (Pointe-Claire, FP Innovations, 2013), Chapter 5 Page 33.
[268] Karacabeyli. CLT …, 34
[269] Karacabeyli. CLT …, 4.
[270] Karacabeyli. CLT …, 4. It is said that up to 1000 mm is not uncommon.

TIMBER JOINTS

11 CASE HISTORIES

Tamedia Office Building – Zurich

Fig. 131. Tamedia Building completed and construction details.

No project better illustrates that the subject of timber joints is inexhaustible, limited only by the imagination of designer, than the Tamedia organisation's office in Zurich, Switzerland (completed 2013). Leading Japanese architect Shigeru Ban, who has earned a worldwide reputation for designing with renewables including cardboard, was given the task of delivering an office building with maximum space utilisation, strong work place appeal for its 480 employees and very importantly, average costs.[271] The building had to be environmentally friendly and have high architectural standards while at the same time contributing to the image of innovation and transparency the company wished to project. The combination of the visible wood structure and the glass facade achieved this.

From previous experience, Ban knew that Swiss timber engineering and workmanship was of a very high standard so his use of timber for its main structural elements was not surprising. The Tamedia building follows two Japanese traditions "Miya-daiku", the refined joints used in temples and shrines and "Sukiya-daiku", traditions from houses and tea rooms which use rustic materials aesthetically. These two influences are "reinterpret[ed] in the light of western influences".[272] The Japanese tradition of carpentry which does not require the use of glue, nails or screws was followed with all the load bearing timber components simply interlocking and using pin connectors. Despite looking back to old traditions, and conforming to the typical architecture of the area, the design is not "old-fashioned". The combination of the visible wood structure and the glass facade is extraordinary.

The precision of CNC milled components allowed 2000 m3 of spruce to be turned into a giant kit making the seven story, 39,000 m^3 building the largest timber framed structure in Switzerland. Two beams sandwich the massive columns, while another perpendicular beam with an oval section that prevents it from rotating penetrates the three elements and locks them together. Economy was achieved by using the timber to its structural limit. The main challenge was the strict Swiss regulations, particularly those relating to fire during construction. "The long lasting collaboration with the authorities was characterised by mutual respect and understanding. The attitude of "together we can do this - even though we don't know how yet" shared by those involved is the premise for the success of such a project."[273]

Tamedia says of their building that "the aim was to make [it] as sustainable as possible. A double facade facing the Sihl river acts as a buffer against climatic conditions as well as a natural ventilation system, and it affords space for meeting rooms and lounges that can be opened up to give onto the river. Wood is a renewable construction material, and its use helped to reduce emissions even during the construction phase. The building will also be operated without CO_2 and will not make any use of nuclear power. Moreover, fossil fuels are eliminated thanks to a futuristic heating and cooling system that utilises the groundwater."[274]

---

[271] World-architects. *Tamedia Office Building*. URL: http://www.world-architects.com/en/projects/41967_Bueroneubau-_Tamedia. Date accessed: 23 August 2016.
[272] Tamedia. *The New Tamedia Building*. URL: http://www.tamedia.ch/en/company/tamedia/the-new-tamedia-building/. Date accessed: 23 August 2016.
[273] World-architects. *Tamedia ...*,
[274] Tamedia. *New ...*,

Fig. 132. Internal views of the completed Tamedia building.

RothoBlass Headquarters, Italy

Fig. 133. Rothoblass headquarters Cortaccia Italy.

Fig. 134. Inside building showing CLT floor and laminated beams

Fig.135. Exterior of building showing cantilevered roof.

The former headquarters of Rothoblass was a conventional building but when the time came to build a new headquarters in Cortaccia, Northern Italy, the opportunity arose to construct a structure showing the use of modern fasteners and membranes in the construction of large timber buildings. By using standard

Rothoblaas product throughout it allowed an easy reference point for the history and performance of all the structural products. The building was designed with the architectural intent of reflecting the main activity of Rothoblaas in the form of a box of screws.

Fig. 136. CLT connection at Rothoblaas headquarters. Fig. 137 Fitting connection to CLT panel..

The envelope of the rectangular building, constructed in three stages between 2004 and 2016 utilises glass on two sides and CLT panels on the other sides. European softwood is used throughout combined with steel columns, some of which are concrete filled for fire resistance. The softwood glue laminated beams are connected with Rothoblaas's own Alubrackets which are a concealed connector. The method of fixing the CLT panels allows the dismantling and reassembly with future expansion.

The facade is mostly clad with vertical wood, Also utilised are Rothoblaas membranes which gives a deeper effect of the facade. The roof is plain and on the south side overhangs 5 m past the wall like an open screw box which allows light in winter and reduces heat in summer. The roof also supports 1000 m2 of solar panels which supply 80% of the energy needed for lighting (LED), power, cooling and warming.

APPENDIX

Recommendation from Galvanisers Association of Australia

Corrosion Zone	Exposure Condition	Minimum Corrosion Protection
Seaspray Zone (C4 &C5)	Enclosed	Galvanised Z275 Class
	Sheltered	Stainless Steel 316 or equivalent
	Exposed	Stainless Steel 316 or equivalent
Coastal Zone (C3)	Enclosed	Galvanised Z275 Class
	Sheltered	**Stainless Steel 316 or equivalent or 600+ gsm Hot Dipped Galvanising**
	Exposed	**Stainless Steel 316 or equivalent or 600+ gsm Hot Dipped Galvanising**
Industrial Zone (C3 or C4)	Enclosed	Galvanised Z275 Class
	Sheltered	Stainless Steel 316 or equivalent (or 600+ gsm Hot Dipped Galvanising if C3)
	Exposed	Stainless Steel 316 or equivalent (or 600+ gsm Hot Dipped Galvanising if C3)
Special Hazard Zone	Enclosed	Special requirements depending on hazard. Refer to corrosion specialist.
	Sheltered	
	Exposed	
Low Hazard Zone (C2)	Enclosed	Galvanised Z275 Class
	Sheltered	Galvanised Z275 Class
	Exposed	Stainless Steel 316 or equivalent or 300+ gsm Hot Dipped Galvanising
Same as TDS35		Different From TDS 35	

SOURCE/OWNERSHIP OF IMAGES

Images not acknowledged are copyright to the author and patent drawings are acknowledged in the text.

1	Failed Joint	Courtesy Deputy Coroner, Coroner's Court of Queensland
2	Schematic of failed joint	Courtesy Deputy Coroner, Coroner's Court of Queensland. Diagram prepared for the Coroner by Mr. Peter Wright
3	Church roof	Queensland Heritage Restorations
4	Cyclone Tracey	National Archives of Australia: A6135, K29/1/75/16
6	7000 year old joint	University of Feiburg (media release)
7	Bronze saw	By Akerbeltz - Own work, CC BY-SA 3.0, https://commons.wikimedia.org/w/index.php?curid=32866357
8	Historical saws	Public domain
9	New traditional joint	Vermont Timber Works
12	British roof joints	Public Domain
13	British joints	Public Domain
14	Japanese gooseneck joint	Chris Hall
15	Japanese locking joint	Chris Hall
16	Bush carpentry	By Bluedawe - Own work, CC BY-SA 3.0, https://commons.wikimedia.org/w/index.php?curid=10828757
17	Bamboo building	Shutterstock
18	Lashed joint	Shutterstock
19	Sons of Gwalia	Greg Meachem
20	Corrosion hazard	Forest and Wood Products Australia
22	Australian bolt	Timber Queensland
24	Z275 bracket	Multinail
25	Test structure	BRANZ
26	Test results	BRANZ
27	Painted bolt	ITW Proline
18	Nail types	Courtesy of Professor Thomas D. Visser.
29	Bronze nail	University of Queensland, RD Milns Antiquities Museum,
30	Nail machine	http://www.tecnofil.net/usato-dettaglio-tecnofil.asp/lang_2/category_12/id_58/wafios-n6.html (Believed to be public domain)
31	Coil of nail wire	OneSteel Wire Pty. Ltd.
32	Spruce Goose	By image http://www.alaska.faa.gov/fai/afss/AcftPhoto-List.htmhttps://www.flickr.com/photos/49487266@N07/7881222436, Public Domain, https://commons.wikimedia.org/w/index.php?curid=33729
33	Nail test	FWPRDC project 02.1209
34	End nailing table	Multinail
36	Nailing truss	Greg Nolan
37	Assembling igloo	Greg Nolan
38	Igloo detail 1	Public domain
39	Igloo detail 2	Public domain
40	Besson's lathe	Public domain
41	Square drive screw	By Library and Archives Canada, Collections Canada website; from Ken Lamb (1998), P.L., inventor of the Robertson screw, Milton

		Historical Society. ISBN 0969562969.; original illustration Peter L. Robertson, 1909 - Collections Canada, Public Domain, https://commons.wikimedia.org/w/index.php?curid=5047078
42	Philips and pozidrive	Control Parts, Lancaster PA.
43	Screw factory	Abbate Screw Products, Inc.
44	Maudsley's lathe	Public domain
58	Joint comparison	Public domain
59	Split ring in operation	Portland Bolt
60	Split ring grooving tool	Portland Bolt
63	Tillamook hangar	Colin MacKenzie
63	Blimps in hangar	Copyright unknown
63	Tillamook hangar construction detail	Colin MacKenzie
63	Tillamook hangar interior view	Colin MacKenzie
64	Truss detail	Redrawn from Navy Department, Bureau Yards and Docks, Lighter-Than-Air Hangar. Drawing 212817 – Library of Congress
65	Split rings	Portland bolt
70	Shear plates	Portland bolt
71	Shear plate assembly	Portland Bolt
72	Tocumwal truss	Greg Nolan
73	Werribee shearplate truss	Owen Peake
74	Truss detail	Public domain
75	Old toothed ring	Public domain
76	New toothed ring	Simpson Strong-Tie
82	Cismon Bridge	http://chestofbooks.com/home-improvement/woodworking/Carpentry-Principles/Section-X-Wooden-Bridges-Viaducts-Etc.html
83	Trajan's Bridge	Attributed to Apollodorus of Damascus - Conrad Cichorius: "Die Reliefs der Traianssäule", Zweiter Tafelband: "Die Reliefs des Zweiten Dakischen Krieges", Tafeln 58-113, Verlag von Georg Reimer, Berlin 1900, Public Domain, https://commons.wikimedia.org/w/index.php?curid=5122586
85	Levittown, PA	Shutterstock
89	Historical nailplates	Photos provided with permission of the Truss Plate Institute (TPI) - www.tpinst.org
90	Historical nailplates	Photos provided with permission of the Truss Plate Institute (TPI) - www.tpinst.org
91	Modern nailplate	Multinail
92	Platern press	Multinail
93	Roller press	Multinail
94	IBM 1130 computer	By Wolfgang Stief from Tittmoning, Germany - IBM 1130, CC BY 2.0, https://commons.wikimedia.org/w/index.php?curid=49057642
95	Incorrect storage	Timber Queensland
96	Joint failure	Timber Queensland
97	Incorrect storage	Multinail
98	Parallel truss press	Multinail
99	Triple grip	Public domain

101	Connector catalogue cover	Simpson Strong-Tie
102	Gun nails on connector	Colin Mckenzie
103	Broken triplegrip	James Pierce
110	Footbridge with diagonal rail	Dennis Clark Photography
116	Breaking line of site	Dennis Clark Photography
119	Cairns handrail	Ports North
119	Split handrail	Copyright unknown
123	Timber rivet	Specialized Timber Fasteners, Canada
124	Typical riveted connection	Specialized Timber Fasteners, Canada
125	Epoxied bolts	Glued Laminated Timber Association
126	Aluminium bracket	Rothoblaas
127	Hook bracket	Rothoblaas
128	Timber office building	Stora Enso (media release)
129	Rothoblaas CLT Bracket	Rothoblass
130	Sherpa CLT Bracket	Sherpa Connection Systems and Siegware Australia
131	Tamedia building	Tamedia
132	Tamedia inside	Tamedia
133	RothoBlass building	RothoBlass
134	RothoBlass inside	RothoBlass
135	RothoBlass external	RothoBlass
136	CLT Connection	RothoBlass
137	Fitting CLT Connection	RothoBlass

WORKS CITED

Anonymous..Founder of Theory – Thomas Tredgold, Engineer *The Telegraph*. March 7, 1929.

Anonymous. Nailing Machine Speeds Building. *Popular Mechanics.* (Chicago. Popular Mechanics, March 1950).

Arch Wood Protection, Inc. and Arch Treatment Technologies, Inc. *Hardware Recommendations for Treated Wood.* June 6, 2006. (No publication details).

Bootle, Keith R. *Wood in Australia, Types, properties and uses, Second Edition*. (North Ryde: McGraw Hill Australia, 2005).

Brunel, Isambard. *The Life of Isambard Kingdom Brunel, Civil Engineer.* (Cambridge: Cambridge University Press, 1870).

Casey, Hugh. *Igloo Type Construction for warehouses, Hangars and Aircraft Hideouts As Developed In Southwest Pacific Area.* This document is a report to the Chief of Engineers , Unites States Army October 21, 1942. Document reference AG 634(10/21/42)E.

Forests and Wood Products Australia. *Manual 6 – Embedded corrosion of fasteners in exposed timber structures.* (Melbourne: Forest and Wood Products Australia, 2007).

Glencross-Grant, Rex, Ian Berger. The European Influence On Laminated Timber Arch Road Bridges In Colonial Australia, 1852-90 In *World Congress On Timber Engineering 2016.*

Gouger, Robert. Memoranda of a Residence in Holdfast Bay Editor Penelope Hop in *The Voyage of the Africane*. (South Yarra: Heinemann Educational Australia, 1968).

Hankins, Alan, Thanh Ho. *Werribee Satellite Aerodrome Hangars – Nomination for Heritage Recognition.* (Engineering Heritage Victoria, 2005).

Haywood D, C. Mackenzie. *Deck Nail Withdrawal Tests FWPRDC project 02.1209.* (No publication details).

Jones, P., E. N. Simons. *Story of the Saw, Spear and Jackson Limited* 1760-1960. (Manchester: Neuman Neame, 1961).

Jureit, J. Calvin in Gang Nails Golden Anniversary, A visit with inventor Cal Jureit and his wife Marie in *Structural Building Components Magazine* September/October 2005.

Karacabeyli, Errol, Brad Douglas, Editors. *CLT Handbook: Cross Laminated Timber US Edition*. (Pointe-Claire, FP Innovations, 2013).

Lampe, Ryan, Petra Moser. Patent Pools: Licencing strategies in the absence of regulation in *History and Strategy* , Edited by Steven Kahl, Michael Cusumano, Brian S. Silverman. (Bingley: Emerald Group, 2012).

LeFever, Gregory. Cut Iron Nails in *Early American Life. (*Firelands Media Group June 2008).

Li, Z.W., N.J. Marston and M.S. Jones. *Corrosion of Fasteners in Treated Timber* Study Report SR241 2011 (Branz, 2011).

Li. Cuoxin, Shanjing Xia, Yilang Peng. Anti-Corrosion Performance of Four Hot Dip Galvanising

Bolts in *Applied Mechanics and Materials Vols. 395-396* (2013).

Louw, Hentie. The Mechanisation of Architectural Woodwork in Britain from the Late-Eighteenth to the Early Twentieth Century, and its Practical, Social and Aesthetic Implications. Part I: The Period c.1790 to c.1860. *Construction History*, (Vol.8, 1992).

Marshall, Colin. Levittown, the prototypical American suburb – a history of cities in 50 buildings, day 25 .*The Guardian* (Australian edition) April 28, 2015

Mason, Matthew and Katharine Haynes. *Adaption Lessons from Cyclone Tracy*. (Gold Coast: National Climate Change Adaption Research Facility, 2010).

National Association of Forest Industries. *Timber Joint Design -3 Bolts, Coachscrews and Timber Connectors.* (NAFI, 1989). (The June 2001 version is available at http://www.timber.net.au/images/downloads/joinery/joint_design3.pdf)

National Association of Forest Industries *Timber Manual Datafile P1 – Timber Species and Properties.* (NAFI).

Newlands, James. *Carpenter and Joiner's Assistant Also A Complete Treatise on Lines.* (London: Blackie and Son, 1880).

Newton, David. *Chemistry of New Materials.* (New York: Facts On File Inc, 2007).

Nolan, Gregory. *The Forgotten Long span Timber Structures of Australia*. A Thesis for the Degree of Master of Architecture, University of Tasmania, 1994.

Nolan, Gregory. Extraordinary Buildings - Wartime design ingenuity with wood in *timber +DESIGN* Autumn 2008.

Oliver, Myrna. *M. Pynoos, 84 Civic Booster, Engineer* in Los Angeles Times July 10, 2002 (obituary).

Pryda. *Pryda Timber Connectors Nailplate Guide*. (Pryda: Dandenong South, 2012).

Raizman. David. *History of Modern Design: Graphics and Products Since the Industrial Revolution.* (London: Laurence King Publishing, 2003).

Rammer, Douglas, Samuel Zelinka, Philip Line. *Fastener Corrosion: Testing, Research and Design Considerations* a paper given at World Conference on Timber Engineering 2006.

Rinke, M. T, Kotnik. The Changing concept of truss design caused by the influence of Science. Structures and Architecture CSA 2010 - *1st International Conference on Structures & Architecture,* July 21-23 2010 Edited by Paulo J. Cruz, S (CRC Press, 2010).

Robinson, John. *Specifiers Manual.* (Carole Park: Industrial Galvanisers, 2013).

Roe, Joseph. *English and American Tool Builders.* (New York: McGraw-Hill, 1920).

Rogers, C, R Thomson, G. Smith. Nailplate Reinforcement of Bolted Joints in *Pacific Timber Engineering Conference 1994*

Rybczynski, Witold. *One Good Turn, A Natural History of the Screwdriver and the Screw.* (New York: Scribner, 2000).

Sauter, David. *Landscape Construction, 3rd Edition.* (Delmar: Cenage Learning, 2011).

Simpson Strong-Tie *Preservative Treated Wood Technical Bulletin No. T-PRWOOD08-R* (Pleasanton: Simpson Strong-Tie, 2008).

Skempton, AW. *A Biographical Dictionary of Civil Engineers in Great Britain and Ireland Volume 1, 1500 to 1830.* (London: Thomas Telford. 2002).

Smith, Joseph. *Explanation or Key to the Various Manufactures of Sheffield.* (Sheffield: Self published, 1816).

Standards Australia. *AS 2334-1980 Steel nails – Metric series.* (Sydney: Standards Australia, 2015).

Standards Australia. *AS1720.1 – 2010 Timber Structures Part 1 Design measures.* (Sydney: Standards Australia, 2010).

Strabo *Geography*

Tampone, Gennaro, Francesca Funis. Palladio's Timber Bridges. *Proceedings of the First International Congress on Construction History, Madrid*, 20th-24th January 2003, ed. S. Huerta, Madrid: I. Juan de Herrera

Timber Development Association. *Massive Timber construction Systems, Cross Laminated timber (CLT).* (Melbourne: Forest and Wood Products Association, 2015).

Timber Engineering Company. *Teco Timber Joint Connectors.* (Washington: Timber Engineering Company, 1936).

Timber Engineering Company. *Manual of Timber Engineering Construction.* (Washington: Timber Engineering Company, 1939)

Timber Engineering Company. *Timber for Recreational Buildings.* (Washington: Timber Engineering Company, 1950)

Timber Engineering Company. *Specify Timber with the TECO System for industrial and Commercial Structures.* (Washington: Timber Engineering Company, 1950),

Timber Engineering Company. *A Brief History of the Timber Engineering Company.* (No publication details, 1958).

Truss Plate Institute. *Design Specifications for Light Metal Plate Connected Trusses TPI 60.* (Miami: Truss Plate Institute Inc, UD).

Ulrich, Roger. *Roman Woodworking.* (New Haven: Yale University Press, 2007).

Wallis, Norman. *Australian Timber Handbook* (Sydney: Angus and Robinson, 1970)

Woodbury, Robert. *Studies in the History of Machine Tools – History of the Lathe to 1850.* (Cambridge: The M.I.T. Press, 1972).

Zelinka, Samuel, Rebecca Sichel, Donald Stone. Exposure testing of fasteners in preservative treated wood: Galvimetric corrosion rates and corrosion product analysis in *Corrosion Science* 52 (2010)

Zarnani, Pouyan, Pierre Quenneville. *Timber Rivet Connection*. (Melbourne: Forest and Wood Products Australia, 2016).

Zelinka, Samuel. Corrosion of Metals in Wood Products in *Developments in Corrosion Protection*, Editor M Aliofkhazraei (InTech, 2014).

Internet Sites

Batchelar, Mark, Ken McIntosh. Structural Joints in Glulam. *New Zealand Timber Design Journal* Issue 4, Volume 7. URL: http://www.timberdesign.org.nz/files/Structural%20Joints%-20In%20Glulam.pdf. Date accessed: 3 January 2017.

Bell, Peter. Continuity in Australian Timber Domestic Building: An Early Cottage in Burra in *Australian Historical Archaeology* 8, 1990. 8. URL: http://www.asha.org.au/pdf/australasian_historical_archaeology/08_04_Bell.pdf. Date accessed: 23 October 2016.

Cook, James. *Captain Cook's Journal*, Tuesday 6th 1769. URL: https://ebooks.adelaide.edu.au/c/cook/james/c77j/chapter3.html. Date accessed: 20 October 2016.

CRC Industries (Aust) Pty. Limited. *Technical Data Sheet Product No. 3013,3014, 3015,3016*. URL: http://www.crcindustries.com.au/assets/files/tds/softseal-3013-tds.pdf Date accessed: 15 December 2016.

Emmick, Tim. *Metal Plated Wood Truss Failure Causes*. Penn State 2012. URL: https://failures.wikispaces.com/Wood+Truss+Failures#Metal%20Plated%20Wood%20Truss%20Failure%20Causes Date accessed: August 10, 2016.

Glued Laminated Timber Association. *Gluelam – Performance Record*. URL: http://www.glulam.co.uk/performance History.htm. date accessed: 2 January 2017.

Kear, G, Hai-Zhen Wu, Mark Jones. The *Corrosion of Metallic Fasteners in Untreated, CCA-, CuAz-, and ACQ-based timbers. Branz Study Report* 153. (Judgeford: Branz, 2006).

Koppers Performance Chemicals. *Lifewood CCA*. 2006.. URL: http://www.kopperspc.com.au/pdf/Lifewood-cca-brochure.pdf. Date accessed: 15 December 2016.

Koppers Performance Chemicals. *Naturwood ACQ*. 2006,. URL: http://www.kopperspc.com.au/pdf/micropro-brochure.pdf. Date accessed: 15 December 2016.

Kruszelnicki, Karl. *Nuts and Bolts – Part 1*. URL: http://www.abc.-net.au/science/k2/trek/4wd/nuts1.htm Date accessed: 2 November 2016.

Lukas Paul. A Twist of Faith An engineer turns an "impossible" idea into manufacturing gold in CNN Money Dec 1, 2002. URL: http://money.cnn.com/magazines/-fsb/fsb_archive/2002/12/01/333852/index.htm Date accessed: 4 December 2016.

Maurer, Libby. Industry veterans Hark Back to Early Plates in Structural Building Components

Magazine, November 2003. URL: http://www.sbcmag.info/article/2003/industry-veteran-hark-back-early-plates Date accessed: 5 August 2016.

McConchie, Matasha. *Five iron nails from the Roman hoard at Inchtuthil* (ANU. UD). URL: http://slll.anu.edu.au/sites/slll.anu.edu.au/files/default_images/McConchie_Classics_Occasional_Paper_1.pdf. Date Accessed: 17 October 2016.

Mason, Matthew and Katharine Haynes. *Case Study: Cyclone Tracy Final Report. U.D.* URL: http://www.riskfrontiers.com/publications/Cyclone%20Tracy%20-%20Report_FINAL.pdf Date Accessed: *29* June, 2013.

Merullo, Roland. J. Calvin Jureit, Inventor Who Transformed Home Building, Dies at 87 Sept. 18, 2005 New York Times. URL: http://www.nytimes.com/2005/09/18/us/j-calvin-jureit-inventor-who-transformed-home-building-dies-at-87.html?_r=0 Date accessed: December 15, 2016.

MiTek. *History*. URL: https://www.mitek-us.com/about/History.aspx. Date accessed: 8 August 2016

Mohammad ,M., Sylvain Gagnon, Bradford K. Douglas, Lisa Podesto. *Introduction to Cross Laminated Timber*, URL: http://www.forestprod.org/buy_publications/resources/-untitled/summer2012/Volume%2022,%20Issue%202%20Mohammad.pdf. Date accessed: 6 January 2017.

Moss, Peter J1 , Andrew Buchanan, Ka Wong. *Moment-Resisting Connections in Glulam Beams*. URL: http://timber.ce.wsu.edu/Resources/papers/9-4-1.pdf . Date accessed: 3 January 2017.

National Archives of Australia *Cyclone Tracy, Darwin – Fact sheet 176*. URL http://www.naa.gov.au/collection/fact-sheets/fs176.aspx Date Accessed: 29 June , 2013.

Nelson, Lee. Technical Leaflet 48, Nail Chronology as an Aid to Dating Old Buildings in *History News*, Volume 24, No 11 (November 1968).

Pryda. *Technical Update Corrosion Resistance of Pryda Products* Feb. 2012, 1. URL: http://www.pryda.com.au/wp-content/uploads/2016/05/Post-Anchor-Guide-MARCH-2012.pdf. Date Accessed: 15 December 2016.

Rhode Island Art in Ruins. HTTP: http://www.artinruins.com/arch/?id=historical&pr=americanscrew Date accessed: 4 December 2016. The site is quoting from *History of the State of Rhode Island with Illustrations, 1878* (Philadelphia. Hoag, Wade & Company. 1878).

Sparvell, Ray. *The Secret History of Nails.* URL: http://www.domain.com.au/news/the-secret-history-of-nails-20160829-gr3b9p/ Date accessed: 21 October 2016.

Stora Enso *Australia's First Wooden Office Built with Stora Enso* CLT. URL: http://buildingandliving.storaenso.com/news/news-and-press-releases/ustralia-office-tora-nso- Date Accessed: 6 January 2017.

Structural Building Component Association. *Industry Timeline*. URL: http://www.sbcindustry.com/content/3/industry-timeline. Date Accessed: 9 August 2016.

Tamedia. *The New Tamedia Building*. URL: http://www.tamedia.ch/en/company/tamedia/the-new-tamedia-building/. Date accessed: 23 August 2016.

Truss Plate Institute. *History*. URL: http://www.tpinst.org/history/ Date accessed: 8 August 2016

Vaccaro, Charlie quoted in Maurer, Libby. Industry veterans Hark Back to Early Plates in *Structural Building Components Magazine*, November 2003. URL: http://www.sbcmag.info/article/2003/industry-veteran-hark-back-early-plates Date accessed: 5 August 2016.

Wells, Tom. Nail Chronology: the use of Technically Derived Features in *Historical Archaeology* 32 (1998). URL: https://uccshes.files.wordpress.com/2012/09/nail-chronology-the-use-of-technologically-derived-features.pdf. Date accessed: December 19, 2016.

Williams, Christopher. Timber Rivets in *Structure Magazine* March 2006, 26. URL: http://www.structuremag.org/wp-content/uploads/2014/09/SF-Timber-Rivets-March-061.pdf. Date accessed: 2 January 2017.

Queensland Building and Construction Commission. *Gun Nailing of Framing Anchors and Straps.* URL: https://www.qbcc.qld.gov.au/blog/tradie-talk/gun-nailing-framing-anchors-straps Date accessed: 4 October 2016.

Queensland Courts, Office of the State Coroner. *Inquest into the death of Annette Lee spencer. URL:* http://www.courts.qld.gov.au/__data/assets/pdf_file/0008/86885/cif-spencer-al-20100628.pdf Date accessed: 19 December 2016.

Queensland Courts, Office of the State Coroner. *Inquest into the death of Isabella Wren Diefenbach.* URL: http://www.courts.qld.gov.au/__data/assets/pdf_file/0019/163027/cif-diefenbach-iw-20120919.pdf. Date Accessed: 15 December 2016.

Timber Preservers Association of Australia *Fasteners in CCA Treated Timber*. URL: http://www.tpaa.com.au/fastenerscca.htm. Date accessed: 25 March 2012.

Visser, Thomas. *Nails: Clues to a Building's History.* University of Vermont, Historic Preservation Research. URL: http://www.uvm.edu/~histpres/203/nails.html. Date accessed; 21 October 2016.

Walker, George. *The Birth of the Cyclone Testing Station*. No publication details URL https://cyclonetestingstation.com.au/existing-content/public/groups/everyone/-documents/advice/jcuprd-045615.pdf date accessed: 5 June 2016.

Willacy, Mark. Child's death increases calls for tougher standards for deck. Australian Broadcasting Commission, *7.30 Report*, April 1, 2014. URL: http://www.abc.net.au/7.30/content/2014/s3976328.htm. Date acessed: 15 December 2016.

Wood Solutions. *Wood durability? Try 7000+ years*. URL: https://www.woodsolutions.com.au/Blog/timber-durability-7000-year-old-wood. Date accessed: 15 December 2016.

World-architects. *Tamedia Office Building*. URL: http://www.world-architects.com/en/projects/41967_Bueroneubau_Tamedia. Date accessed: 23 August 2016.

ABOUT THE AUTHOR

Ted Stubbersfield was born in the small Queensland town of Gatton in 1950. After studying to be a pastor in Brisbane and the UK he returned to the family business, Gatton Sawmilling Co. A fair question would be, "Can anything good come out of Gatton"? Well, Gatton was the home of a Governor General of Australia (William Vanneck 1938). It is also the home of the best and most innovative hardwood producer in Australia, Outdoor Structures Australia (OSA).

The family had been involved in sawmilling and building for about 140 years and a lot of knowledge has passed through the generations. In 1985 we ventured into the footbridge market (almost by accident) and then followed public landscaping. Initially, we just did as we were told by consultants who knew very little about timber. In about 1988 Ted decided he would come to know the medium he was working with far better than any of his competitors and most of the professionals who used his products.

Ted realised that there were no useful standards and guides for designing and building weather exposed timber structures such as boardwalks. That led in 1997 to his first formal research project on boardwalk design, engineering supply and construction. Over the years there followed a complete set of guides. These allowed professionals to design timber structures of exceptional beauty and durability. Typically, everybody wants to re-invent the wheel and the guides were usually ignored. Invariably, the same mistakes keep being made over and over. This little book is an attempt to remedy this.

In 2012, the time came to close the manufacturing arm of OSA and to take on a less stressful lifestyle. Ted plans to put in writing much of what he has learnt so the industry does not have to relearn it. This book on Timber Joints is the ninth in a series of Timber Design Files that are intended to show designers how to avoid the pitfalls of common, but often bad practice as well as Standards that can be very inadequate and engender a false sense of security.